merchants

children

festivals

magicians

How to read this book

explorers

plague

Entries are listed alphabetically. If you prefer to, you can find which page someone or something is on by looking in the index starting on page 123.

everyday life

sport

Words followed by* - you can look up what they mean in the glossary on page 122.

ships

battles

Names in **bold** in the text are of people who have their own entry. The little number in the margin beside them shows which page you'll find them on.

parishes

plots

royals

On the next page, there's a time chart showing how major people and events were connected.

painters

poor people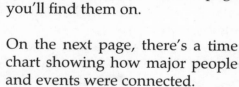

churchmen

books and writers

nobles and statesmen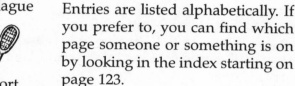

When?

1485   Battle of Bosworth. Henry Tudor defeats Richard III and becomes Henry VII, the first Tudor king.

1486   Henry VII marries Elizabeth of York.

1487   Lambert Simnel pretends to be the Earl of Warwick.

1491   Perkin Warbeck pretends to be Richard of York.

1497   John Cabot discovers Newfoundland.

1501   Prince Arthur marries Catherine of Aragon.

1509   Henry VIII becomes King of England and marries Catherine of Aragon.

1513   Battle of Flodden between England and Scotland.

1515   Thomas Wolsey becomes Chancellor.

1516   Thomas More writes *Utopia*.

1517   Evil May Day riots in London.

1520   Field of the Cloth of Gold.

1525   William Tyndale translates the New Testament.

1529   Cardinal Wolsey loses power and Thomas More becomes Chancellor.

1533   Henry VIII marries Anne Boleyn.

1534   Act of Supremacy. Church of England breaks with the Pope.

1535   Thomas More executed. Miles Coverdale translates the whole Bible.

1536   Anne Boleyn executed. Henry VIII marries Jane Seymour. Act of Union unites England and Wales.

1539   Dissolution of the larger monasteries. Henry VIII marries Anne of Cleves, then divorces her and marries Catherine Howard.

1542   Catherine Howard executed.

1543	Henry VIII marries Catherine Parr.
1547	Henry VIII dies. Edward VI becomes king with Duke of Somerset as Protector.
1553	Edward VI dies. Lady Jane Grey becomes queen for nine days and then Mary becomes queen.
1554	Mary marries Philip IV of Spain.
1555	Richard Chancellor arrives in Moscow. Bishops Latimer and Ridley are burned.
1556	Archbishop Cranmer burned.
1558	Mary dies. Elizabeth I becomes Queen.
1563	Thirty-Nine Articles become law. Foxe's *Book of Martyrs* published.
1565	Mary Queen of Scots marries Lord Darnley.
1566	David Rizzio murdered.
1567	Earl of Bothwell murders Darnley and marries Mary Queen of Scots.
1568	Mary Queen of Scots flees to England.
1576	First theatre in London opened by James Burbage.
1580	Francis Drake returns from his voyage round the world.
1583	Throgmorton Plot to kill Elizabeth I.
1584	Walter Raleigh sets up first English colony in North America at Roanoke Island.
1586	Babington Plot uncovered by Walsingham.
1587	Mary Queen of Scots executed.
1588	Armada defeated by the English fleet.
1590	First Shakespeare plays are staged.
1593	Christopher Marlowe killed.
1596	Water closet described by James Harrington.
1598	Battle of Yellow Ford. Irish defeat the English.
1601	Earl of Essex executed.
1603	Death of Elizabeth I.

animals
creatures similar to people

Tudor towns were full of animals. Our streets are empty by comparison. In Tudor times, you could hardly walk outside your door without bumping into some other species.

Wandering pigs were a problem. They were always escaping from backyards, and were often allowed out to scavenge. A pig is a large animal and can be dangerous. They sometimes bit small children.

HELP!

Town chicken 'farmers' used to keep hundreds or even thousands of birds in their cellars and attics. It was quite common to keep hens in the bedroom.

Herds of cows were driven through the streets to the 'shambles' behind the butchers' shops.

Then of course there were horses. They were everywhere. In 1581, on the road between Shoreditch and Enfield just outside London, a gentleman called Sir Thomas Wroth counted 2,100.

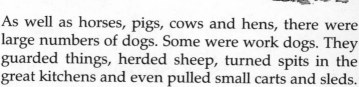

1,974 – WILL THIS NEVER END?

As well as horses, pigs, cows and hens, there were large numbers of dogs. Some were work dogs. They guarded things, herded sheep, turned spits in the great kitchens and even pulled small carts and sleds. Others were posh pets. Posh pets tended to be hounds, spaniels and lap dogs. Mongrels and the rest were unposh.

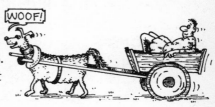

WOOF!

🫖 Anne of Cleves
royal wife who became a sister
1515-57

62 Anne of Cleves, a German princess, was **Henry VIII's** fourth wife. Before they met, Henry saw a
64 flattering portrait of her by **Hans Holbein**, but when

she arrived in England in December 1539, the reality didn't match up. She wasn't very pretty, she couldn't speak English and she couldn't sing or play a musical instrument. He called her 'the Flanders mare'. The marriage was declared null and void in July 1540 and Anne spent the rest of her days in England living off a pension from Henry and with the title of 'King's sister'. Thomas Cromwell who arranged the marriage was executed.

Armada
big fleet that failed
1588

84 **Philip II** of Spain wanted to turn England back into a Catholic* country and to stop English support for his rebellious Protestant* subjects in the Netherlands, then part of the Spanish Empire. In May 1588, a mighty Spanish invasion fleet, or 'Armada', of 138 ships set sail. The plan was to sail up the Channel to the coast of Flanders, in what is now southern Belgium. There they would meet up with the invasion barges of a Spanish army of around 30,000 men, ready to cross the Channel and invade England. There would be an uprising of English Catholics to back them up.

Delayed by storms, the Armada had a long, uncomfortable crossing. The sailors slept on deck because their ships were crammed with 19,000 extra soldiers. It wasn't until 29 July 1588 that they were finally spotted, off Lizard Point in Cornwall. **Sir Francis Drake**, second-in-command of the English fleet, was based at Plymouth in Devon at the time. When news of the sighting reached him, he's said to have calmly finished his game of bowls before putting to sea.

Top commander of the English fleet was **Charles Howard**. He could count on the advice of brilliant captains such as **Frobisher**, **Hawkins**, and of course Drake, in his Council of War. The English plan was to avoid sailing too close to the Spanish. There would be strictly no boarding - this was to be a long-range sea battle, the first of its kind. The English would rely on their big guns and on the fact that their ships were easier to steer than the Spanish ships. 'Long range' is a relative term - in those days, guns were inaccurate beyond 200 metres. They also became red hot if fired more than once every five minutes.

11

Howard's fleet picked off the Spanish ships all the way up the Channel. By 6 August, the battered Armada was anchored off Calais, where they were due to meet up with the invasion army from the Netherlands. Next night (7/8 August), the English launched fire ships. The Spanish broke anchor in order to escape the flames. In the morning the English smashed them while they were still disorganised. What was left of the Armada escaped by sailing right round the north of Scotland and Ireland. A third of them sank in dreadful weather. In total, 15,000 Spaniards died.

Arthur, Prince of Wales
prince who died young
1486-1502

61 Arthur was the eldest son of **Henry VII**, the first Tudor king. He was named after legendary King Arthur to show that the Tudors traced their descent from early British kings. Negotiations for his

21 marriage to the Spanish princess **Catherine of Aragon** began when he was two. The marriage

finally took place in 1501 when he was fifteen, although the couple were thought to be still too young to live together as man and wife. Less than five months after the marriage, Arthur died of consumption, the old word for tuberculosis. Catherine went on to marry Arthur's brother who by then had become King Henry VIII. The rest, as they say, is history.

KOFF! KOFF!

CONSUMPTION

Babington Plot
scraping the bottom of the barrel
1586

72 From 1568, **Mary Queen of Scots** had been imprisoned at Chartley House in Staffordshire. In 1586 nearly twenty years later, her English supporters planned to start a Catholic uprising
42 backed by a foreign invasion. **Elizabeth** was to be murdered and Mary would become Queen. Sir Anthony Babington, a rich young Catholic, wrote letters to Mary for the plotters. The coded letters were smuggled in and out of Chartley in waterproof leather packets hidden in the bottom of beer barrels.

DID YOU HAVE TO DRINK THE ENTIRE BARREL TO GET AT THE MESSAGE?!

HIC!

117 Unknown to the plotters, **Walsinghams's** agents opened all the packets, deciphered the letters and then resealed them and sent them on. In his letters, Babington described the plan, including the plan to murder Elizabeth. As soon as Mary gave her approval to Babington (29 July), the authorities pounced.

58 Babington was **hung, drawn and quartered** at Tyburn on 20 September 1586. Mary Queen of Scots was beheaded on 8 February 1587.

🐕 beds
comfy things to sleep in

Ah, bedtime at last! A straw pallet and a nice, comfy log for a pillow. Well - not neccessarily. In country areas a straw pallet for a mattress and a log for a pillow were still common, and servants nearly always slept on straw, but the Tudor age was an age of increasing comfort for many others. Those who could afford to began to buy feather mattresses and pillows.

The standard bed was a four poster, hung with thick curtains to keep out the night air. Night air was

thought to be dangerous. Few people slept alone. Usually they had at least one bed companion and more if they were small children. Even royal princes and princesses shared their beds with special companions.

Servants often slept at the foot of their master or mistress's bed, on a 'truckle bed' - a collapsible bed which could be stored under the great bed in the daytime.

beer
It was better than water

Imagine a world without, tea, coffee or fizzy drinks. Where the water is dirty and dangerous to drink, and where fruit juices are almost unknown. You could get thirsty.

The Tudor answer to this problem was - beer. Strong beer because it tasted nice and it made you drunk if that was what you wanted, and weak 'small' beer because it was safer than water. The reason beer is safer than dirty water is because the alcohol in beer kills off harmful bacteria. Not that the Tudors knew about bacteria.

42
62 Everyone drank beer, including children. **Elizabeth I** always drank small beer for breakfast. When **Henry**

VIII sent an army to help Spain against France in 1512, his army mutinied because the Spanish served wine and not beer (although wine would have done just as well). In 1542, an army which he'd sent north to attack Scotland refused to move for nine days because the beer hadn't arrived!

> WE WANT BEER!

> NOW!

> GIVE US OUR BEER!

Boleyn, Anne
queen who lost her head
1507?-1536

62 Anne Boleyn was the second wife of **Henry VIII**. She wasn't especially pretty, in fact she had a sort of sixth finger on her left hand and her enemies said that she had three breasts. But she was funny and lively and when she first arrived at Henry's court in 1522, men swarmed round her like bees round a honey pot - Henry VIII included.

In order to marry Anne, who was Protestant*, Henry 21 broke with his first wife, **Catherine of Aragon**, who was Catholic*. The Pope refused to agree to the split, so Henry broke with the Pope and started the Church of England with himself as its head. Henry and Anne were married on 25 January 1533. By that time Anne was already several months pregnant 42 with the future **Elizabeth I**.

But Henry wanted a son to inherit his crown. Anne duly obliged him in January 1536 - but the baby boy was stillborn. Henry was fed up with her. She was charged with being unfaithful to him with four other men including her own brother, charges which were probably untrue. She was arrested in May and, after a short trial, her head was cut off by an expert swordsman brought over from France.

HMM, C'EST BIEN TRANCHANTE!

⚔ Bosworth, Battle of
where the Tudors triumphed

1485

The Battle of Bosworth ended the Wars of the Roses* and started the rule of the Tudors. It was fought between Henry, Earl of Richmond, soon to become **Henry VII**, who was on the Lancastrian side of the Wars of the Roses, and Richard III who was on the Yorkist side.

On 1 August 1485, Henry landed at Milford Haven, in Wales, with an army paid for by the French king. He had tried to invade once before, in 1483, but had

17

been driven back by bad weather. From Milford Haven, he marched east across the Midlands. He met Richard's army at Bosworth about twelve miles west of Leicester on 22 August. Richard fought bravely but some of his leading supporters changed sides at the last moment. He was thrown from his horse and killed in a bog. When the battle was over, Richard's body was either dragged naked behind a horse or carried to Leicester across a horse's back with a noose round his neck, depending on which account you read. Henry VII was crowned on 30 October.

Bothwell, James Hepburn, Earl of
muscular earl who kidnapped a queen
1535?-1578

James Hepburn, Earl of Bothwell, was strong as an ox and wild as a lion. A mad, bad Scottish earl if ever there was one. He's famous for being the third
72 husband of **Mary Queen of Scots**.

Bothwell became a member of Mary's privy council in 1561. After various adventures, including escape to France following a quarrel with the truly mad Earl of Arran, Mary took a liking to him - especially after
90 the gruesome murder of her secretary **David Rizzio**

(1566), which was backed by her husband, drunken **Lord Darnley**. Bothwell had sided with Mary.

In 1567, Bothwell murdered Darnley and blew up the house where Darnley was staying in Edinburgh. By that time Bothwell and Mary were probably lovers and Mary may well have known about plans for the murder. He then 'kidnapped' her (with her agreement) and arranged for a quickie divorce from his previous wife. They got married and Scotland was scandalised. There was a rebellion, naturally. Mary was captured by the rebel lords and ended up in prison in England. Bothwell fled to Denmark where he too was imprisoned. After five years, he went properly mad and died.

Cabot, John (Giovanni)
he found Newfoundland
around 1425-1500

John Cabot is famous for discovering North America for the English. He was an Italian adventurer and merchant who, before moving to Bristol (around 1495) had traded as far as the Black Sea and may have visited Mecca in disguise. Like Christopher Columbus, he worked out that, because the world is round, it should be possible to travel to Asia by sailing west across the Atlantic. Bristol was a good place to start from because Bristol merchants were an adventurous lot who had experience of sailing the Atlantic. It's very possible that men from Bristol had sighted the 'Isle of Brasil' (Newfoundland) even before Columbus landed in the Caribbean in 1492.

Cabot set sail on 20 May 1497 in the *St. Matthew*, a small ship with a crew of around twenty men. A month later, on 24 June, they reached what was probably Newfoundland and there they raised the banner of **Henry VII**. They sailed within a bow shot of the shore but didn't land and were back in Bristol fifteen days later. On the basis of this adventure, Cabot gave lectures at court and became known as the 'Great Admiral'. In 1498 he set out again with a fleet of five ships and two hundred men. They reached America and may have sailed as far south as the Caribbean, but some of the ships sank in bad weather and Cabot himself probably died on the voyage.

SO THERE I WAS, JUST OFF SHORE..

Catherine of Aragon
Catholic queen who married twice

1485-1536

[62] Catherine of Aragon married **Henry VIII's** elder [12] brother, **Prince Arthur** then the heir to the throne, in 1501. He was fifteen and she was sixteen and they were thought to be too young to live together as man and wife. Arthur died in 1502 so they never did.

Seven years later, on 11 June 1509, she married Henry VIII. Catherine and Henry lived together happily for many years but unfortunately, of Catherine's six babies, only one, the future Queen [74] **Mary**, survived. Henry needed a male heir to inherit his throne. Giving up on Catherine, he fell in love [16] with his next wife, **Anne Boleyn**. On 14 July 1531 he slipped out of Windsor Palace without saying goodbye and he never saw Catherine again.

Henry tried to pressurise Catherine into accepting that their marriage had never been a proper marriage in the first place. The reason he gave was that she had once been married to his brother Arthur - this is forbidden by the Bible. Bit by bit, her servants and even most of her furniture were taken away from her until eventually she was living almost in one room, and was in fear of being poisoned. But still she refused to agree. The Pope backed her up. In order to divorce her without the Pope's agreement, Henry broke with the Roman Catholic* Church and set up the Church of England with himself as its head. He married Anne Boleyn in 1533. Catherine died three years later.

I MUST EAT...

BUT IT MAY BE POISONED!

Catherine Parr
she outlived a legend

1512-48

62 Catherine Parr was the sixth and last wife of **Henry VIII**. (Henry was *her* third husband.) When he first suggested marriage she was terrified by the very idea (small wonder) and said: 'It would be better to be his mistress than his wife.' But Henry, being king, got his way and they were married on 12 July 1543.

Catherine was small but she was clever, 'pregnant with wittiness' as she was described at the time. As queen she looked after the education of the future **Edward VI** and **Elizabeth I** and also protected her stepdaughter, the future Queen **Mary**. After Henry died in 1547, she married Thomas Seymour, brother of **Edward Seymour, Duke of Somerset**. She'd been planning to marry him back in 1543 before Henry stepped in. When she died the following year after giving birth to a baby girl, she was still only thirty-six but with four husbands behind her. In 1782, her lead coffin was opened and a cut made in her arm. The flesh was found to be still moist and white although later it rotted.

FORSOOTH- A MIRACLE! THE FLESH IS MOIST & WHITE!

Cavendish, Thomas
he circled the world

1560-92

When he was a teenager, Thomas Cavendish, a rich young man, wasted most of his inheritance on luxury living. In order to recover his fortunes, he sailed on the first expedition to found an English colony in North America (1585), organised by **Sir Walter Raleigh**. They captured some Spanish ships and Cavendish returned home with a decent profit, but not enough to keep him in the style to which he'd become accustomed.

His next voyage took him right round the world, the second voyage round the world by an

Englishman (the first being by **Sir Francis Drake** 1577-80). His three ships and 123 men set out from Plymouth in July 1586. They burned Spanish towns on the Pacific coast of South America and captured several rich Spanish ships. From South America they crossed the Pacific and Indian oceans and rounded the Cape of Good Hope east to west landing back in England in 1588 a few days after the defeat of the Spanish **Armada**. Of the three ships, only Cavendish's flag ship, the *Desire*, made it home - but the voyage was still hugely successful. Cavendish was rich once more.

WHERE'S CAVENDISH?

FALLEN OVER, I THINK.

GOOD RIDDANCE!

But not for long. Being Cavendish, he squandered his money. In 1591 he set off from Plymouth yet again, this time with five ships. His last voyage was a disaster. He quarrelled with his officers and seems to have gone slightly mad before turning for home. He died at sea.

Cecil, Robert
1st Earl of Salisbury
powerful elf who planned for peace
1563-1612

Robert Cecil was tiny, no more than 5ft 3 inches tall (roughly 1.5 metres) and slightly hunchbacked. **Elizabeth** used to call him her 'little elf'. He had a pet parrot which he taught to dance on his dining table but not any real friends - he was too cool for that.

25 Like his father **William Cecil**, the most important of all Elizabeth's ministers, Robert was hard working and very, very clever. When William died in 1598, Robert became the most powerful man in the kingdom. Elizabeth was old so he planned for the peaceful succession of James I. And when Elizabeth finally died (1603), James kept his 'pygmy' on as Secretary of State.

THE QUEEN IS DEAD. LONG LIVE THE KING!

Cecil, William, Lord Burghley
seriously sensible secretary
1520-98

When he was an old man, William Cecil advised his
24 clever son **Robert Cecil**:

Serve God by serving the Queen, for all other service is bondage to the devil.

It was the path which he himself followed. When
42 **Elizabeth I** came to the throne in 1558 she immediately made Cecil her Principal Secretary of State. From that time on, he never lost her trust. Elizabeth wasn't an easy woman to work for but she

was charming and he was loyal and both were very clever, so the partnership worked. Also they agreed about things: in particular both were moderate Protestants* who wanted to avoid war with Catholic* Spain and with France if possible. The partnership lasted for forty years - until Cecil died. One of the most successful political partnerships in English history.

In 1571, Cecil was made Lord Burghley. He became extremely rich and built three large, expensive Tudor mansions: Theobalds in Hertfordshire, Burghley in Lincolnshire and Cecil House in London. The old nobility, including Elizabeth's favourite **Leicester**, looked down on him and were jealous of his power. But Elizabeth backed him up. When he was weak and lying on his death bed, she fed him herself with 'her own princely hand'.

Chancellor, Richard
he made it to Moscow
died 1556

In 1553, Richard Chancellor was appointed 'pilot general' of an expedition under Sir Hugh Willoughby to seek a northeast passage to China across the freezing sea to the north of Russia. He was already an experienced navigator and had voyaged to North America in 1550.

In May 1553, the little fleet set out from England, but they were separated in a storm off the north coast of Scandinavia. Willoughby was forced to land in Lapland, where he and his crew died in the extreme cold. Meanwhile Chancellor made it across the White Sea in his ship, the *Edward Bonaventure*. He landed and travelled overland to Moscow, where he was warmly welcomed by Ivan the Terrible, the first Tsar of Russia.

WHAT A COLD LAND!

Chancellor and the Tsar agreed to start a trading relationship between Russia and England. The **Muscovy Company** was founded in 1555 to start the trade, after Chancellor returned to England. He set off again and by October he was back in Moscow. The return journey of 1556 was a disaster. Out of four ships, two were sunk off the Norwegian coast, one failed to reach England until 1557 and Chancellor's *Edward Bonaventure* was wrecked off the Scottish coast. Some of the crew made it to shore but he himself was drowned.

77

🧒 children
beast-like beings bettered by beating

Tudor children had to respect their parents - or suffer the consequences. Even when grown up, they were expected to stand up in the presence of their parents unless permitted to sit down. They had to call them 'Sir' or 'Madame'. Children ate at a separate table. They had to serve their parents at table if there were no servants to do it.

Methods for bringing up children were basically the same as for animals. They were seen as unformed adults who had to be trained. Bad ideas and behaviour must be beaten out of them. In fact, beating was thought to be good for them. None of this means that parents didn't love their children, or children their parents.

HURRY UP, LAD.

chimneys and windows
letting smoke out and light in

The common people in Tudor England ate reasonably well but their houses were miserable hovels. A one-room cottage was the norm. If they could afford it they built extra rooms called 'outshuts'. Not for them, new-fangled gadgets such as windows with glass in them or chimneys to let the smoke out.

Before the Tudor period the smoke from fires had to find its way out as best it could, perhaps through a hole in the ceiling. People actually thought that smoke was good for them, that it toughened them up as it did the timbers. Chimneys must have made a huge difference to the quality of life. Rich people built big, fancy chimneys to show off to the neighbours.

Big glass windows were another new fashion for those who could afford them. Who wanted dark, dank rooms lit by arrow slits? Hardwick Hall was one of the new-style Tudor houses. There was a rhyme about it:

> *Hardwick Hall,*
> *More glass than wall*

Together with new plaster ceilings, as opposed to wood, the whole feeling of the smart, new Tudor houses of the rich was lighter and more comfortable than what had gone before.

clothes
all laced up

Everyone wore the same type of underclothing - a smock or shift. But above that clothes were different depending on class and occupation. Medieval 'sumptuary' laws, which tried to control who wore what depending on how important they were, were still in operation, and servants and country people tended to wear drabber and more old-fashioned clothes than people who lived in the cities.

The rich wore some of the most outrageous garments ever worn. And getting dressed was no simple matter. There were no buttons. Everything had to be pinned or laced. They used their clothing to show off their wealth. Outer garments were deliberately 'slashed' so that rich inner garments could peep through. Jewels were sewn into cloth. Lace, a very expensive material, was worn in abundance.

Tudor men dressed like peacocks. There was a cult of the male leg. Some men even wore padding beneath their tights to enhance the shape. As for the cod piece which jutted from their pantaloons, nothing quite like it has been seen since! Short cloaks were fashionable, often made of perfumed leather.

Women's fashions were as extreme as the men's. The basic garments were a separate skirt and bodice but these were very fancy. At the front of the bodice was a 'stomacher' which was stiffened with canvas or pasteboard and sometimes with bone. The stomacher pushed the stomach in and the breasts up. It descended to a point and as the century went by this point fell lower and lower.

Skirts were worn shorter than on the continent. A Spanish courtier who travelled to England with Philip II in 1554 was shocked by the shortness - he could see women's ankles! As the century wore on, skirts grew wider and wider. By the end of **Elizabeth's** reign, they were held out at the sides by the farthingale, a word which comes from the Spanish word *verdugado* (a hooped skirt). A stiff hoop frame was worn beneath the skirt jutting out from the hips all round. This held out the skirt which then fell vertically to the ground.

Starch came into fashion in the 1570s. By Elizabeth's time, huge starched ruffs jutted from the neck.

'A VERY LARGE RUFF'

Common Prayer, Book of

an uncommonly beautiful book

1549

The *Book of Common Prayer* was mainly written, or

33 prepared, by **Thomas Cranmer** and contains some of the most beautiful writing in the English language. It grew from the 'Act of Uniformity', passed by Parliament in 1549. The idea was to make sure that everyone followed the same 'uniform' Protestant* version of Christianity. As part of this, the new *Book of Common Prayer* was ordered to be used in all churches. Riots and rebellions against it broke out in Devon and Cornwall. A revised, more Protestant version was brought out in 1552.

Mary abolished the *Book of Common Prayer* and went back to the old, Latin rituals.

42 **Elizabeth** brought out a revised version, in a new Act of Uniformity in 1559.

32

Coverdale, Miles
Bible translator who lived abroad ✝
1488?-1568

Miles Coverdale was the first person to translate the whole Bible into English. He was a Protestant* and a friend of Thomas Cromwell. In 1528, he had to leave England to escape accusations of heresy - of having opinions very different to what was expected by the established church - and while abroad he helped 113 **William Tyndale** with his great translation of the New Testament, the second part of the Bible, the part which deals with the life of Christ and his disciples. Perhaps on the strength of this experience Coverdale was asked to translate the entire Bible by a Dutch printer based in Antwerp (1534). Unlike Tyndale's translation, Coverdale's is not from the original Greek and Hebrew but from later German and Latin versions.

✝ Cranmer, Thomas
bishop who wrote a book
1489-1556

In 1533, Thomas Cranmer was made Archbishop of 62 Canterbury by **Henry VIII**. He was a Protestant* so he was happy to help Henry to divorce his first wife, 21 Catholic **Catherine of Aragon** - and to set up the Church of England as a separate church with Henry at its head instead of the Pope. His *Book of Common*

Prayer for the new church (first issued 1549) contains some of the most beautiful writing in the English language.

Unfortunately for Cranmer, Catherine of Aragon's daughter **Mary** came to the throne in 1553. Cranmer was immediately imprisoned. Under terrible pressure and in fear of death, he signed six 'admissions' agreeing that the Pope was the head of the English church after all. He was then 'degraded' - stripped of all his bishop's robes and his hair cut short. Finally he was sentenced to be burned.

On the day of his death, Cranmer took back all the 'admissions'. He then ran to the stake in Oxford so fast that others could hardly keep up with him. When the flames were lit he thrust his right hand (which had done the signing) into them and said: 'This hand hath offended'.

Darnley, Lord Henry Stuart
short-lived husband from hell

1546-67

In February 1565, tall, athletic Lord Darnley headed north to Scotland to woo **Mary Queen of Scots**. He was a Catholic*; she was a Catholic. She was beautiful; he was handsome. He was nineteen; she was twenty-two. Soon after his arrival, Darnley got measles. Mary nursed him. They were married that July.

Darnley was a husband from hell. He was proud and stupid and he drank too much. Mary turned to her Italian secretary **David Rizzio** for support. Mad with jealousy, Darnley agreed with some Scottish lords that Rizzio must be murdered. On the evening of 9 March 1566, Rizzio was dragged from Mary's supper chamber at Holyrood Palace. Darnley's dagger was the one left sticking in his side.

Mary and Darnley now loathed each other. Mary fell in love with the dashing, dangerous **Earl of Bothwell**. However, when Darnley fell ill the following January, he and Mary seemed to make it up. On the evening of 6 February 1567, Mary made him comfortable in a lonely house just outside Edinburgh. That night the house was blown apart by a massive explosion - arranged by Bothwell. Darnley and a servant were found lying under a tree. They'd been strangled. It was just under two years since he'd first arrived in Scotland.

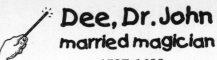

Dee, Dr. John
married magician
1527-1608

Dr. Dee was interested in astrology*, alchemy* and magic. Everyone believed in magic in those days. 42 **Elizabeth I** set the day of her coronation by Dee's astrological calculations.

When he was quite elderly, Dee met a man called Kelly. Kelly always wore a black cap - to disguise the fact that his ears had been cut off for forgery. Kelly warned that a spirit called *Lundrumguffa* was out to destroy Dee and Dee was so impressed that the two men teamed up. From 1583-87, they travelled widely around the courts of Europe. Then in April 1587, a spirit (not *Lundrumguffa* but another one) told Kelly that the two men should share their wives. Dee agreed but only reluctantly. Bitter quarrels soon followed and the two men parted company. Dee returned to England where he eventually died in poverty.

A VISION OF LUNDRUMGUFFA

✝ Dissolution of the Monasteries
when monks were made miserable

62 **Henry VIII** became 'Supreme Head on Earth of the Church of England' in 1534. In a sense, from that

moment everything belonging to the Church now belonged to him. All religious houses were inspected by government agents to see if the monks were living properly - or living too well. The fact was that many monasteries were not quite what they ought to be. Some monks kept mistresses and fine wine cellars and generally lived it up. An *Act for the Dissolution of the Lesser Monasteries* was passed and during 1536 they had to surrender all their wealth to the crown. In 1539, an *Act for the Dissolution of the Greater Monasteries* was passed. They too had to surrender their wealth. Thomas Cromwell was the minister who dreamed up the 'Dissolution'.

Monasteries were then almost the only place where poor people could go for medical treatment and for other types of care. The Dissolution caused great suffering among the poor - and for the monks. Large gangs of unemployed monks roamed the 103 countryside as **beggars** for years afterwards. But Henry and many others made a lot of money. Today the landscape of England is littered with the ruins of these once great buildings.

Drake, Sir Francis
sea dog who sailed against Spain
around 1540-1596

In 1494, by the Treaty of Tordesillas, Pope Alexander VI divided the newly discovered world outside Christian Europe into two halves. One half went to Catholic* Spain and the other half went to Catholic Portugal - which didn't seem very fair. As Francis I of France put it:

Show me the clause in Adam's will which gives the King of Spain dominion over half the world.

Francis Drake, a tough Devon sea captain and a staunch Protestant*, didn't think it was fair either, especially since the Spanish executed Protestants if they found them in 'Spanish' waters. His life's work was to fight Spanish rule outside Spain. Of all his hugely profitable voyages, that of 1577-80, when he was the first Englishman to sail right round the world, was the most important. When he returned home to Plymouth in September 1580, his little flagship, the *Golden Hind*, was weighed down to the gunnels with Spanish treasure.

In 1587, **Elizabeth I** put him in charge of an expedition to harass the Spanish **Armada** in port before it could set sail for England. Drake sailed right into Cadiz harbour and destroyed around eighty enemy ships. He wrecked another hundred ships along the coast. He had 'singed the King of Spain's beard'. This expedition delayed the start of the Armada and gave the English time to prepare their defence. When the Armada finally set sail, Drake was vice-admiral of the fleet which defeated it. He was buried at sea after yet another expedition to Spanish America, in 1596.

Dudley, Robert, Earl of Leicester
nobleman loved by Liz
1533-88

Robert Dudley was handsome, athletic and noble. **Elizabeth I** made him her 'Master of Horse' in 1559 shortly after she became queen - and promptly fell in love with him. They were the same age and they'd known each other since childhood. Robert stayed her favourite throughout his life although no one knows if they were ever lovers. In 1564 she made him Earl of Leicester.

Robert himself was married twice. First to Amy Robsart who died after falling down stairs in 1560. Gossip accused him of having her murdered so that he could marry Elizabeth. More likely, she fell because she was weakened by breast cancer. In 1578 he secretly married Lettice Knollys, the widowed mother of **Robert Devereux, Earl of Essex**. Elizabeth never forgave the 'She Wolf' as she called Lettice - but she forgave Robert.

In 1585, she made him commander of her army fighting the Spanish in the Netherlands. He was a failure, mainly because he was too conceited to get on with his commanders. Elizabeth forgave him yet again, but by now he was middle-aged. He'd grown rather fat and red in the face. He probably died of malaria.

East India Company
they made it rich

established 1600

'Companies' of merchants established by royal charter were a sixteenth century invention. They were a way of increasing the power and wealth of a country by using private money. The 'Governor and Company of Merchants of London Trading into the East Indies' were granted its royal charter by

Elizabeth I on 31 December 1600. In the charter, Elizabeth granted the 'East India Company', as it was later called, the right to make and enforce laws in its territory. It was also granted a monopoly on trade - in other words, no one else was allowed to trade in its patch.

To start with, the main aim of the 'Company', and of its leading investor the Earl of Cumberland, was to muscle in on the profitable spice trade from the far east. In 1600 this trade was controlled by the Portuguese and the Spanish. The Company soon became very strong and rich. It had its own private army. By the late seventeenth century it ruled a large chunk of India.

Edward VI
young king who caught consumption

1537-53

62 Young Prince Edward was **Henry VIII's** only male
95 heir. His mother was **Jane Seymour**, Henry's third and favourite wife. When Henry died in January 1547 (when Edward was only nine), Edward was crowned ahead of either of his two elder sisters,
74
42 **Mary** and **Elizabeth**, because he was the only boy.

He was clever and a keen Protestant*. During his
33 reign, **Cranmer's** beautiful *Book of Common Prayer*

was published. But he was far too young to rule personally. To start with, the kingdom was governed by his uncle **Edward Seymour**, Duke of Somerset - the 'Lord Protector', but in 1549 the reins of power were taken over by John Dudley, Earl of Warwick and the Duke of Northumberland. Somerset was executed.

Edward caught consumption (tuberculosis) in January 1553, a fatal illness in those days, as it often is today. News of his death was hidden from the public for several days so that Warwick could put his own doomed daughter-in-law, **Lady Jane Grey**, on the throne.

IS HE DEAD YET?

Elizabeth I
queen who married her country
1533-1603

Elizabeth's father was **Henry VIII**. Her mother was **Anne Boleyn**. On 19 May 1536, her father executed her mother. No wonder Elizabeth never married.

Elizabeth was a Protestant* like her mother and her half brother **Edward VI**. This meant that she was reasonably safe while her father and then her brother ruled but was in danger once her Catholic* sister **Mary** came to the throne (1553). Mary imprisoned her in the Tower of London and she narrowly escaped with her life.

She became queen in 1558 when Mary died, and she ruled for forty-five years, steering her mainly Protestant country through Catholic plots and plans for invasion. Along the way she defeated the Spanish Armada, executed her Catholic cousin, Mary Queen of Scots and made the Church of England the moderate Protestant church which it still is today. She was no fanatic. What people believed in private was their own affair. As she put it:

I shall not open windows into men's souls.

Elizabeth was very clever and charming but she had a temper and could swear like a trooper. She would sometimes bat her ministers round the ears if they annoyed her, even **William Cecil** her most important minister.

She wore incredibly rich clothes and insisted on being adored by all the handsome and brilliant men who flocked to her court. Probably she would have liked to marry one of them, **Robert Dudley Earl of Leicester**, but that would have caused trouble with the others so she didn't. Her greatest love was England itself.

🫖 Elizabeth of York
kind queen of cards

1465-1503

Elizabeth was Queen of Hearts - and Diamonds, and Spades, and Clubs. She's the queen whose picture often appears on playing cards. She was the wife of

61 **Henry VII** the first Tudor king.

Elizabeth was a Yorkist, one of the two sides in the Wars of the Roses* which split England in the fifteenth century. Henry was a Lancastrian. When they were married the two sides were united and the Wars of the Roses were finally over. She was beautiful, kind and cheerful. Henry loved her and they were happy together. They had eight children. Four died as infants, but one of them grew up to be

62 **Henry VIII**. Henry VII never remarried after she died.

🥣 enclosures
common theft

The wealth of Tudor (and medieval) England grew

42 on the backs of sheep. By **Elizabeth I's** time there were three times as many sheep as people on the land. Trade in woollen cloth had doubled between 1500 and 1600. But there was a price to pay - sheep needed more and more land for grazing.

In order to increase the size of their flocks, wealthy families 'enclosed' common land with hedges or fences. This process had started in the twelfth century but it reached its peak in Tudor times. Once enclosed, only the sheep of the family which did the enclosing were allowed to graze there. But the common land had been just that - land held in common by the village, where all the villagers had the right to graze their animals and to grow crops in season. Due to enclosures, large numbers of villagers lost everything. They had no choice but to join the armies of **sturdy beggars** who roamed the country stealing and poaching to get food. There's a rhyme about it:

103

The law locks up the man or woman
Who steals the goose from off the common;
But leaves the greater villain loose,
Who steals the common from the goose.

Essex, Robert Devereux, Earl of
favourite who went too far
1566-1601

42
39 **Elizabeth I** loved to surround herself with handsome, clever men. **Robert Dudley** was the one she loved best. But after he died in 1588, Robert Devereux became her favourite, perhaps because he

45

was Dudley's stepson. Robert Devereux was charming but hasty. He charged through life like a whirlwind. He used to shovel down breakfast and then throw on whatever clothes came to hand. He was very tall and prowled Elizabeth's court 'like the neck of a giraffe'.

Their relationship was stormy. Several times Elizabeth boxed his ears and once he even drew his sword on her. But always she forgave him - until he went too far. In 1599, having failed dismally in his command of her army in Ireland, he rushed back to London and burst into her bedchamber spattered in mud from his wild gallop across England. He was desperate to explain himself. She had her wig off and was looking old and tired. She wasn't happy.

After that, Essex was imprisoned in his London mansion for months on end while Elizabeth tried to decide what to do with him. He gathered a group of discontented young men around him. On 8 February he broke out and roamed the streets of London with a troop of around two hundred followers, calling for a general uprising. No one joined him and he was forced to surrender. It took three blows of the axe to chop his head off.

Evil May Day

what a riot!

1517

During the sixteenth century, London was home to a growing number of foreigners, either craftsmen with special skills to sell or foreign traders. On May Day in 1517, the London apprentices rioted against the foreigners. No one was killed so it was quite a mild

62 riot compared to many both before and since. **Henry VIII's** reaction was far from mild. Thirteen 'poor younglings' were hanged. 400 others were let off but they had to walk past him with nooses round their necks. 'Evil May Day' was called 'evil' because of Henry - not because of the riot.

exploration

carving up the cake

Under the Treaty of Tordesillas (1494) the Pope divided all the new lands of the world outside Christendom between the Spanish and the Portuguese. It was Tudor government policy,

42 especially under **Elizabeth**, to win part of this enormous cake for England. Brilliant sailors such as

38
60
56 **Francis Drake**, **John Hawkins**, **Martin Frobisher** and

23 **Thomas Cavendish** sailed west into the unknown.

88 **Walter Raleigh** worked to establish an English

colony in North America. **Anthony Jenkinson** and **Richard Chancellor** pushed east across Russia and towards China.

The voyages of these remarkable men, and many more, were recorded by a writer called Richard Hakluyt. His greatest book *The principall Navigations, Voiages and Discoveries of the English Nation*, first published 1589, is still worth reading today.

festivals
feasts, fights and frolics

There were no holidays as we know them today in the Tudor period but there were plenty of festivals when everyone took the day off. Puritans disapproved but it was another hundred years before most of the old festivals were banned. At all of them there was drinking and dancing, and usually sports and fighting as well. May Day was one of the wildest. The colourfully decorated Maypole would be dragged to the place of festivity and raised up vertically to shouts and cheers. Round it the young men and women drank and cavorted till late at night.

Each locality had its own favourite festivals. In Coventry and Reading, Hock-Tide, the week after Easter, was big. On Hock Monday the men grabbed the women and held them to ransom. On Hock Tuesday, the women grabbed the men. Robin Hood days were popular too. **Hugh Latimer** once found that no one came to hear him preach because it was a Robin Hood Day. In fact, many people knew more about Robin Hood than they did about religion.

Field of the Cloth of Gold
where monarchs met
1520

In June 1520, **Henry VIII**, with 5,000 followers, crossed the English Channel and set up camp near Calais. The French king Francis I, also with a huge band of followers, set up his own camp nearby. But this wasn't for battle. This was a 'friendly' meeting. Each king tried to outdo the other with the magnificence of his camp. Temporary palaces and tents were put up in fields. One tent was made of 'cloth of gold', whence the name.

From 7-24 June, wine and other expensive drinks flowed from fountains, there were jousts and other entertainments. All was fun and revelry. Fun which

49

was only slightly spoiled by the fact that the two sides couldn't understand each other properly. The two kings were still young - Francis was twenty-six and Henry was twenty-nine. They had a wrestling match. Henry lost.

⚔ Flodden, Battle of
a sad day for Scotland
1513

On 22 August 1513, King James IV of Scotland, husband of **Henry VIII's** sister Margaret, invaded England at the head of an army of 30,000 men. Henry was at war with France. Scotland and France were allies, so James was only doing what he'd promised. An English army of 20,000 men rushed north. English and Scots met in battle on 9 September on *Flodden Field* in Northumberland. There the Scots were totally out-classed by the English archers and foot soldiers. James and thirteen of his earls were killed along with 10,000 others, the 'flowers of the forest' as Scottish poets later described them.

62

food

meat and sweetmeats

Tudor breakfast was a simple meal. Often just a slice of bread and a glass of beer, taken in the bedroom while getting dressed.

The big meal of the day was dinner. This usually started around noon (earlier in the country). For those who had the time and the money it was a long drawn out performance put on to impress guests and neighbours. Diners sat in strict order of importance and children weren't allowed to join in. (They ate separately.) A very large, fancy salt cellar was placed in the centre of the table. What mattered was to sit 'above the salt'. Important guests sat on the same side of it as the host, thus the expression. Most diners sat on benches. Chairs with backs were for the master and mistress and a few important guests only.

In posh households the food was brought in by a long line of servants in a sort of procession. There might even be musicians to accompany them.

Table manners were very different to today. Wooden bowls had been replaced by tin and pewter and even silver, but forks were hardly known. A knife and fingers makes for greasy hands so there was an 'ewer' of water on the table for washing between courses. Tudor manners were strict, in a manner of speaking:

Pick not thy teeth with a forkette, for it hurteth.

Touch not any parte of the meate, saving that which thou wilt cut of, for thy selfe.

Scratche not thy head with thy fingers when thou arte at thy meate; nor spitte you over the table-boorde.

The favourite food of the gentry was whole joints of beef and mutton with bread to soak up the gravy and washed down with beer. There might be side dishes of game or other meats. They ate a much wider variety of animals than we do today. On Fridays everyone who could afford to ate fish - by law. To protect English fishermen, **Elizabeth** passed a law commanding all her subjects to eat fish twice a week. Either way, fish and meat were the centre of every smart meal. Raw fruit and vegetables were looked on with suspicion because water was unclean and therefore dangerous:

Beware of green salletees and rawe fruytes for they will make your soverayne sick.

The main courses were followed by the sweets. Usually pasties or jellies but sometimes incredible sculptures made of sugar. The Tudors had very sweet teeth and no idea of the connection between eating sugar and tooth decay. Elizabeth's teeth went black, rotten in her old age, and the same thing happened to many other Tudors.

WOULD YOU LIKE A LITTLE SWEETIE?

MMM!

While the wealthy dined on meat and more meat and followed it up with delicious sweets, the poor made do with broth, porridge, dairy products and bacon. Their bread was often made of rye or barley. When times were really tough they might make bread from acorn flour. But they still had their beer to wash it down.

Because there was no electric light, people tended to get up earlier and go to bed earlier than we do today, so as to make the most of the daylight. So supper was at five or before. This allowed the better off a couple of hours to go hunting, visit the theatre or friends or some other leisure activity during the afternoon. Most people went back to work of course.

football

when the ball was boiled

Football was popular in Tudor times, although the 'foot' bit is rather misleading since players were free to use their hands as well. The wooden ball, often of box, yew or holly, was boiled in fat to make it slippery and was just small enough to be held in the hands. Players cropped their hair and beards short so the other side couldn't get a grip on them. Mostly the game was at least played on foot, but some games of 'football' were played on horseback - with clubs up to a metre long, more like polo in fact. Often entire villages or even districts fought each other. The gentry mucked in with the yokels.

THAT'S THE WAY! GO FOR THE MAN WITH THE BALL!

The level of violence was truly appalling by modern standards. Small packs of men would roam the fields looking for their opponents - with or without the ball. Few matches passed without broken heads or limbs. A foreigner watching a game in 1588, the year of the Armada, commented:

> *If this be but playe, I cold wish the Spaniards were here to see our plaies in England. Certes they would be in bodilye feare of our warre!*

There were traditional days for football. Shrove Tuesday, the day before the first day of Lent, was popular. At Ashbourne in Derbyshire the game went on all day and the goals were three miles apart! It was said that up to two thousand players took part.

Foxe's Book of Martyrs
persecuted Protestants' publication

'That huge dunghill of your stinking martyrs, full of a thousand lies'.

Okay, so not everyone liked John Foxe's famous *Book of Martyrs*, especially not Catholics*. Mainly however, it's not full of lies but of truth, if one-sided. The English translation of Foxe's *Actes and Monuments of the Latter and Perilous Dayes* to give it its full name, soon called *Foxe's Book of Martyrs*, was published in 1563. It's an account of the cruelties of the Inquisition and of the sufferings of English Protestant* martyrs from the fourteenth century onwards. In particular it describes the near three hundred burnings during **Mary's** reign.

By the time it was published, **Elizabeth** was securely on the throne and the dark days of Mary's reign were over. Elizabeth ordered that a copy should be set up in every church as a reminder. For the next hundred years, it was the most widely read book in England after the Bible.

Frobisher, Sir Martin
seriously strong sailor

around 1535-1594

Martin Frobisher was one of the toughest Tudor sea dogs. He was very strong - he once lifted an Inuit plus canoe out of the water single handed - and he was a brilliant and brave sailor. He was also a pirate and was arrested five times between 1559 and 1576, although never brought to trial - perhaps because he tended to prey on Catholic* shipping.

Between 1576 and 1578 Frobisher made three voyages in search of a northwest passage to China around the coast of America. He never found it (there isn't one) and all he brought back was tons of fool's gold (iron pyrites). But he was the first European to explore into the Arctic Circle in that region.

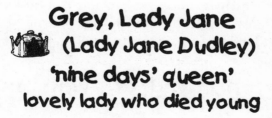

After his voyages to find a northwest passage, he went back to piracy which was more profitable than exploring. He was knighted for his part in defending England against the Spanish **Armada**. After years of further adventures, he died from wounds taken in a battle on the French coast.

Grey, Lady Jane
(Lady Jane Dudley)
'nine days' queen'
lovely lady who died young

1537-54

Lady Jane Grey had royal blood in her veins. She was first cousin to **Edward VI**, who was young and sickly and wasn't expected to last long. That royal blood was her problem. Her father forced her to marry nobleman Guildford Dudley, intending that, through her, his friends the Dudleys would become the next royal family of England when Edward died. Jane loathed her in-laws. The Dudleys were cruel. They used to pinch and hurt her.

Guildford's father persuaded Edward to make Jane his heir, rather than his sister **Mary** who was Catholic*. When Edward died (June 1553), Jane became the new queen. She fainted when she was told the news. She reigned for just nine days and during that time she absolutely refused to allow Guildford to be made king. The Dudleys were furious. Not that it made any difference. Mary marched into London and Jane and Guildford were both thrown into the Tower of London. On 12 February 1554, Guildford was beheaded first and then Jane.

hanging, drawing and quartering
a highly unpleasant punishment

There was quite a lot of hanging, drawing and quartering in the Tudor period. It was the traditional punishment for High Treason. Briefly, it involved:

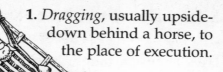

1. *Dragging*, usually upside-down behind a horse, to the place of execution.

2. *Hanging* - but not till dead.

3. *Drawing* of the guts from the still living victim.

4. *Burning* of the guts in front of him.

5. *Chopping* the head off. At least he was now definitely dead.

6. *Quartering* of the body so that bits could be displayed around the kingdom as a warning to others.

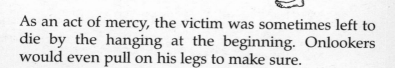

As an act of mercy, the victim was sometimes left to die by the hanging at the beginning. Onlookers would even pull on his legs to make sure.

Hawkins, Sir John

skilful sailor who also sold slaves

1532-95

John Hawkins was a tough, West Country seaman from Plymouth, where many Tudor sailors came from. He was the first Englishman to trade in slaves from Africa to America. Since only the Spanish and Portuguese were allowed to trade with America, he took a risk on his first big voyage (1562). His second voyage (1564) was backed by **Elizabeth** and was very profitable. His third voyage (1567) was a disaster due to Spanish treachery.

In 1577 Hawkins was made treasurer of the navy. Due to him, new, faster ships were built. They had more space for guns and for the seamen, who were better paid. Hawkins' new ships were very important when it came to defeating the great Spanish **Armada** in 1588. He died at sea during another attack on Spanish settlements, in the West Indies.

Henry VII

Careful king who started the Tudors

1457-1509

Henry VII's grandfather was a Welshman called Owen ap Meredith ap Tudor. 'Ap' means 'son of' in Welsh. Due to his descent from Edward III on his mother's side, Henry became the senior *Lancastarian* claimant for the throne of England during the Wars of the Roses*. In 1485 he invaded England from exile in France and beat the *Yorkist* King Richard III at the **Battle of Bosworth**. Five months later he married the Yorkist **Elizabeth of York**, thus uniting Lancastarians and Yorkists and ending the Wars of the Roses for good. It was a happy marriage.

Henry VII was clever and very careful with money. He used to read and sign every line of the royal accounts. When he came to the throne, England was weak and divided. By the time he died it was peaceful and prosperous - and the Tudors were firmly on the throne.

ONE GUINEA, FIVE SHILLINGS, THREEPENCE HA'PENNY AND ONE FARTHING PLUS TWO GUINEAS, THREE SHILLINGS, SIXPENCE AND A FARTHING, THAT MAKES...

Henry VIII
big man who married a lot
1491-1547

Henry VIII was the second son of **Henry VII**. His elder brother **Arthur** died when Henry was eleven. When Henry VII also died (1509), Henry got the crown that should have gone to Arthur. He also got Arthur's widow, whom he married, a young Spanish princess called **Catherine of Aragon**.

Henry VIII was hugely popular when he came to the throne. He was tall, athletic, handsome and clever. He loved music, dancing, hunting and books. When he died he was still popular, but he was hugely fat and constipated and had to be hauled up and down stairs with a winch.

He had six wives. Three of them were called Catherine, two were called Anne and one was called Jane, in order: Catherine of Aragon, **Anne Boleyn**, **Jane Seymour**, **Anne of Cleves**, **Catherine Howard** and **Catherine Parr**. What happened to them is best remembered by the rhyme: 'Divorced, beheaded, died - divorced, beheaded, survived'. He had three legitimate children: **Mary** by Catherine of Aragon, **Elizabeth**, by Anne Boleyn, and **Edward** by Jane Seymour.

A big man, Henry had a big impact on England. Among other things: he broke with the Catholic* church and started the Church of England with himself at its head, he **dissolved the monasteries** and took their money, and he built up the Royal Navy so that it was the most powerful navy in Europe.

Hilliard, Nicholas
a miniature painter

around 1547-1619

Around 1570, Nicholas Hilliard was appointed 'limner' and goldsmith to **Elizabeth I**. 'Limner' was the Elizabethan word for a painter of miniature portraits and Hilliard was the best miniature painter of them all. His paintings are like little jewels, only a few centimetres across. Some of them are painted on the backs of playing cards. He was very much an English painter because, as he put it:

Rare beauties are ... more commonly found in the isle of England than elsewhere.

63

Holbein, Hans
portrait painter plagued by Puritans
1497-1543

Hans Holbein was a German portrait painter who moved to England towards the end of his rather short life. It was difficult to make a living in Basle where he lived, due to the activities of extreme Puritans. They disapproved of painting. He stayed in London for eighteen months (1526-8) and painted superb portraits of English men and women, also of German merchants living in London. Then he returned to Basle, where in 1529 many of his paintings were destroyed in Puritan riots. Life was impossible, so in 1532 he returned to England. He died of the plague before he could return home to Basle, where he had hoped to end his days.

PURITAN!

Howard, Catherine
young queen who lost her head
?1520-1542

62 Pretty Catherine Howard was the fifth wife of **Henry VIII**. Henry spotted her in 1540 when she was a maid of honour (and first cousin) to his then wife
9 **Anne of Cleves**. On 9 July of the same year Anne was set aside by Henry and on the 28th he married Catherine.

Catherine was probably only still in her teens but she
33 had already been engaged twice. **Cranmer** told a shocked Henry about his wife's colourful past. Her

former fiances Francis Dereham and Thomas Culpepper (who was also her cousin) were then tortured. It seems that she was probably unfaithful to Henry with Culpepper *after* she became queen, although Culpepper denied this to the bitter end. Both Dereham and Culpepper were executed and Catherine was beheaded in the Tower of London, on the same spot where another of Henry's wives, **Anne Boleyn**, had been beheaded six years earlier.

Howard, Charles, Lord of Effingham
sensible Lord Admiral
1536-1624

Charles Howard was a handsome Tudor nobleman, first cousin to **Elizabeth I** herself. In 1585 he was made Lord Admiral and in 1587 Elizabeth put him in command of naval defences against the mighty Spanish **Armada** which was gathering for the invasion of England. Better seamen, such as **Drake**, **Hawkins** and **Frobisher**, were available, but being a nobleman, Howard's command would be accepted by all without envy.

Howard was no fool. He asked Drake, Hawkins and Frobisher to be in his council of war and he listened to their advice. When the time came, the Armada was smashed.

Jenkinson, Anthony
he tried to trade with China
died **1611**

Anthony Jenkinson made four amazing voyages to Russia and lands beyond (1557-60, 1561-4, 1566-7 and 1571-2). He opened up the then unknown territory of Central Asia to European eyes, for the first time since the days of Marco Polo nearly three hundred years earlier. The first journey (1557-60) took him around the coast of Norway to the White Sea then overland to Moscow where he dined with Tsar Ivan the Terrible. From there he travelled down the Volga to the Caspian Sea, then overland, arriving in distant Bokhara after countless adventures. He was hoping to open a trade route to China but Bokhara was too lawless to travel further and he had to turn back. He returned safely to Moscow and then to England.

His second voyage took him to Moscow again and then south to Persia. He was hoping to make a trade agreement with the 'Great Sophi', as the Shah of Persia was called in England. The Shah nearly had him killed as an 'infidel' (non-Muslim) but later allowed him to go. There was no trade agreement.

⁷⁷ The third and fourth voyages were also to Moscow, on business for the **Muscovy Company**.

Jonson, Ben
top Tudor playwright
1572-1637

Ben Jonson's stepfather was a bricklayer. When he left school, Jonson tried his hand at bricklaying before he became an actor and a writer. He was one of the greatest playwrights of his time after ⁹⁶ **Shakespeare**, who was a friend. In fact Shakespeare is said to have been an actor in Jonson's comedy *Every Man in His Humour* (1598), the play which made Jonson famous. Further successes followed, such as *Volpone* and *Bartholomew Fair*. They contain some wonderful poems such as *Drink to me only with thine eyes* (in *Volpone*).

Having been a bricklayer, Jonson was probably quite tough and strong. In 1598, he killed a fellow actor in a duel. He narrowly escaped hanging by pleading

'benefit of clergy' (clergy could not be hanged by a civil court). In Tudor times, you were a 'clergyman' if you could read Latin from a Bible. He was however branded as a criminal.

In later life Jonson put on shows at the court of King James I.

Kyd, Thomas
a very bloody playwright
1558-94

Thomas Kyd's play *The Spanish Tragedie* was written some time between 1584-9. It started a fashion for bloodthirsty plays about murder and revenge. The blood was peppered with plenty of ranting speeches - 'the swelling bombast of bragging blank-verse' as another writer described the style. *The Spanish Tragedie* was the most popular play of its time. Kyd followed it with at least four other plays and probably several more.

71 Kyd was a friend of **Christopher Marlowe** and shared lodgings with him in 1591. Marlowe was suspected by the government of being an atheist - someone who didn't believe in God - a crime in those days. In 1593, Kyd's rooms were searched and 'atheistical' papers were found there. Under torture he said that the papers belonged to Marlowe. He died shortly after.

Latimer, Bishop Hugh
Protestant bishop who lit a candle

around 1485-1555

62 Hugh Latimer was a Protestant* who advised **Henry VIII** on how to get rid of his Catholic* wife
21 **Catherine of Aragon**. He was good friends with two other leading Protestants, Thomas Cromwell and
33 **Thomas Cranmer**.

41 During the reign of **Edward VI**, Latimer became a famous preacher, but he was arrested (1553) after
74 Catholic **Queen Mary** came to the throne. He and fellow bishop Nicholas Ridley were burned at the stake in Oxford on 16 October 1555. His last words to Ridley, as the flames were lit:

> *Be of good comfort Master Ridley. We shall this day light such a candle, by God's grace in England as I trust shall never be put out.*

Leicester, Earl of *see* **Dudley, Robert**

long galleries
somewhere to walk in wet weather

A new fashion in big houses during the Tudor period was the long gallery. Usually it stretched the whole

length or breadth of the house. It was a place for the family and their guests to stroll and take their exercise on rainy days. The walls were usually covered in wood panelling and perhaps with tapestries as well. Ceilings were often plastered rather than being of dark wood as in the old days.

make-up
things to do with the face

The ideal look for a Tudor woman was a white skin, hardly any eyebrows or eyelashes, a smooth, high forehead and fair hair.

Ladies would bleach their hair by sitting in the sun - but then they had to watch out that their faces didn't go brown! A face mask kept in place by a button held between the teeth did the trick.

MMPHF!

A really white skin needed more than the absence of sunlight. Some whiteners were very bad for the skin. Favourites included a powder made of ground alabaster, beeswax, asses' milk, and ground-up pigs' jaw bones. Another whitener was white lead with vinegar, and sulphur. **Elizabeth** wore it and in later life her complexion was terrible.

Spots and freckles were treated with ground

42

brimstone, sublimate of mercury or oil of turpentine. All of which were also very damaging.

To repair the damage, cheeks (and breasts) might be glazed with egg whites. Blue veins were then painted over.

For the fashionable look, lips were a splash of vivid red against white skin. They were painted with cochineal (made from beetles), earth pigments or mercuric sulphide.

Eyelids were darkened with kohl, such as is still used in the Middle East. Eye pupils could be made to dilate with drops of belladonna (deadly nightshade).

Marlowe, Christopher
one in the eye for literature
1564-93

On 30 May 1593, twenty-nine year old writer Christopher Marlowe was stabbed in the eye following an argument in a tavern in Deptford. The blow was probably to the eye, the 'brains coming out at the dagger point' according to the man who killed him. It wasn't the first time Marlowe had been in trouble. Back in 1589, he'd spent time in prison following the death of an innkeeper's son in a brawl. And in the year of his death he had been deported from Holland for trying to use forged money.

But Marlowe was far more than a dangerous adventurer. He probably worked for **Elizabeth's** secret service - and he was the greatest Tudor playwright after **Shakespeare**. His first play, *Tamburlane the Great* (1587), changed the face of Tudor theatre. It must have been very exciting - and dangerous too. In an early showing, a pregnant woman and her child were killed when a gun aimed at the 'Governor of Babylon' misfired. Other masterpieces followed: *The Tragical History of Doctor Faustus* (1588?), *The Fabulous Tragedy of the Rich Jew of Malta* (1589), *The Massacre at Paris* (1591) and *The Troublesome Reign of Edward II* (1592).

Before he died, Marlowe was accused of atheism and blasphemy. Not believing in God was a serious crime in those days - if he hadn't been murdered, the government probably would have arrested him.

Mary Queen of Scots
a captivating case of Catholicism
1542-87

Mary was a week old when her father, James V of Scotland died and she became Queen of Scotland.

When aged six she was shipped over to France and engaged to be married to Francis, the heir to the French throne. She was brought up as a French woman.

They married in 1558. Next year, Francis inherited his crown and Mary became Queen of France as well as Scotland. A year after *that*, Francis II died and Mary was a widow at eighteen. She decided to return to the Scottish kingdom which she could hardly remember.

Mary's Scottish reign was a disaster. She married her second husband, **Lord Darnley** in 1565, but he turned out to be a drunken, murderous fool. He helped in the murder of her Italian secretary **David Rizzio** and was then murdered himself. Mary capped it all by marrying his murderer, the **Earl of Bothwell**. She was probably in love with Bothwell. The shocked Scottish lords forced Bothwell to flee and locked up Mary in the island castle of Loch Leven. From there she escaped to England.

Unfortunately, Mary had also claimed that she was the rightful queen of England, through her grandfather **Henry VII**. This displeased her cousin **Elizabeth I**. She spent the next nineteen years in prison, where she was at the centre of several Catholic plots to murder Elizabeth. Finally Elizabeth had her executed.

🫖 Mary I
'Bloody Mary'
Catholic queen who burned bishops

1516-58

Mary Tudor became queen of England in 1553 when she was thirty-seven. Her face was worn, she had no eyebrows and she spoke with an unusually deep voice. Life had been difficult. She was the eldest child of **Henry VIII**, by his first wife, Catholic* **Catherine of Aragon**. After Henry divorced Catherine and married Protestant* **Anne Boleyn**, Mary was declared illegitimate. Anne Boleyn was a dangerous enemy and may even have planned to poison her 'stepdaughter'. As it was, Mary was forced to be lady-in-waiting to her younger sister, Anne Boleyn's daughter the future **Queen Elizabeth I**.

62
21
16
42

Mary was a Catholic like her Spanish mother. When she became queen in 1553, she tried to force England to become Catholic too. She married **Philip II** of Spain (1554) which sparked a Protestant rebellion. In the following years nearly three hundred Protestants were burned at the stake including **Thomas Cranmer**, Nicholas Ridley and **Hugh Latimer**.

84
33
69

Horror at the burnings earned her the nickname 'Bloody Mary'.

Mary had several 'phantom' pregnancies - when her stomach swelled and she thought she was pregnant - but no real pregnancies. She died childless, thus paving the way for Elizabeth to come to the throne.

Medina-Sidonia, Alonzo Perez de Gusman el Bueno, Duke of

seasick admiral who led the Armada

1550-1619

Alonzo Perez, Duke of Medina-Sidonia, was a mighty Spanish nobleman and one of the richest men in Europe. In 1588, **Philip II** of Spain made him commander of the soon-to-be-launched **Armada** against England. Alonzo tried to refuse, saying that he knew more about gardening than war, but Philip insisted.

The Armada was a disaster for the Spanish, partly because Alonzo knew nothing about ships and he suffered terribly from sea sickness. Despite the defeat, Philip continued to trust him. In fact he remained in control of the Spanish navy for many more years.

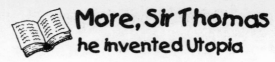

More, Sir Thomas
he invented Utopia

1478-1535

Sir Thomas More was honest, clever and funny - 'born for friendship' in the words of his friend Erasmus. He wrote a brilliant book called *Utopia*, a word which he invented, about a country where people live peacefully and are free to disagree with each other (published 1516). **Henry VIII** was very fond of him - for a while.

In 1529, when **Cardinal Wolsey** fell from power, More became Lord Chancellor. Two years later, Henry VIII finally split with his first wife **Catherine of Aragon** and started the Church of England with himself at its head. More was opposed to all of this. He opposed Henry's marriage to **Anne Boleyn** (1533) and refused to go to her coronation. Henry was furious.

Next year More was locked up in the Tower of London. He was tried on trumped-up charges. Among his judges were the father, the brother and the uncle of Anne Boleyn. Unsurprisingly, he was found guilty and beheaded.

LET'S SEE NOW, GUILTY OR NOT GUILTY?

GUILTY, I SHOULD SAY, DEFINITELY.

YES WHY NOT - GUILTY!

Morton's Fork
taxman's choice

From 1486 until his death in 1500, John Morton was
61 the most powerful man in England after **Henry VII**.
He was Archbishop of Canterbury, a Cardinal and
Henry's Chancellor. Henry was very strapped for
cash at the start of his reign and one of Morton's jobs
was to raise money for him.
'Morton's Fork' was one way of
going about it. Men who were
obviously rich were told that they
could afford to pay more tax;
those who appeared to be poor
were told that they were hiding
their wealth. Morton became
very unpopular but Henry
liked him.

THAT'S A FAT
STOMACH FOR A
POOR MAN!

£ Muscovy Company
they failed to find a passage

established 1555

In 1553, Sir Hugh Willoughby and
26 **Richard Chancellor** set out to
discover a northeast passage
by sea around the north coast
of Russia to China. Willoughby
died in the attempt. Chancellor
ended up in Moscow, where he
met the first Russian Tsar,
Ivan the Terrible. Ivan agreed
to start a trading relationship
with England.

HAVE WE GOT
A DEAL?

DA!

As a result of Chancellor's voyage, the Muscovy Company was founded in 1555 by Sebastian Cabot, son of the famous explorer **John Cabot**. The other backers were a group of London merchants. The Company was granted a monopoly on trade with Russia, but its other purpose was to continue the search for a northeast passage. It never found a northeast passage but it traded profitably for more than two hundred years.

¹⁹

music
unruined by recording

One of the saddest things about the modern world is how we've lost the habit of singing and whistling in public. In Tudor times the streets were full of music.

Manual labourers and mechanical artificers keepe such a chanting and singing in their shoppes.

Everyone was expected to know something about music. The children of gentlemen were brought up to be able to sing and play. They would have been appalled by our modern ignorance. Music was popular with the highest in the land. **Henry VIII** was a good musician as was **Elizabeth I**. When young, Henry used to practise the lute, virginals and organ 'day and night'.

Elizabeth granted the exclusive right to print and sell music to the joint organists of her Chapel Royal, Thomas Tallis and William Byrd. They happen to be two of the greatest English composers.

One of the most popular forms of music was the madrigal. Several singers would sing poems unaccompanied, their voices weaving together and falling apart in rich, complicated patterns.

Norfolk, Thomas Howard, Fourth Duke of

Catholic peer who married a lot
1536-72

Thomas Howard, Duke of Norfolk was top nobleman in Elizabethan England and the only duke. He married and was widowed three times. By inheriting his wives' fortunes, he became the richest man in the country. Clever marrying seemed to be the best way to stay ahead.

HMM- WHO SHALL I MARRY NEXT TIME?

72 In 1569 Norfolk secretly agreed to marry **Mary Queen of Scots** who was then imprisoned in England. He and Mary would rule Scotland, and if
42 **Elizabeth I** died without an heir, Mary would inherit the crown of England too. A Catholic* uprising in the north of England in support of this plan was brutally defeated by Elizabeth's army. To be fair, Norfolk himself was a Protestant* and he didn't take part in the uprising. But he was arrested anyway. Released the following year, he promised never ever to marry Mary.

No such luck. He then backed the conspiracy of
89 Italian banker Roberto **Ridolfi**. Ridolfi planned for a Spanish army to overthrow Elizabeth and put Mary on the throne. Part of the plan was that - Norfolk should marry Mary! Norfolk was tried as a traitor and executed on Tower Hill.

O'Neil, Hugh
Lord of Tyrconnel
'the Great Earl'
Irish rebel who rode to ruin

around **1540-1616**

Hugh O'Neil led the last great Irish rebellion against English domination before the beginning of the twentieth century. In 1598 he won the title of 'the O'Neil' - the top lord of northern Ireland. That same year he smashed an English army at the Battle of Yellow Ford on the Blackwater River in Armagh. This victory triggered a general uprising against the English throughout Ireland, but instead of seizing the leadership of the uprising, O'Neil dithered. A large English army under the **Earl of Essex** landed in Ireland the next year and - both men dithered.

SHALL I ATTACK?..

PERHAPS BETTER NOT...

BUT THEN AGAIN...

ALL RIGHT - ATTACK!

-BUT THEN...

Essex was replaced by Lord Mountjoy. Meanwhile Catholic* Spanish forces landed at the port of Kinsale to support the Irish. Mountjoy beseiged the Spanish in the port. He smashed O'Neil and his rebel army when they came to rescue the Spanish.

Two years later O'Neil submitted to the English and the rebellion was over. He was allowed to keep his lands but he couldn't live with the disgrace. In 1607, he and other northern chiefs set sail for Spain. The 'Flight of the Earls' marked the end of Gaelic Ireland.

parishes
the locus of local government

The Parish was the basic unit of government of Tudor England. Everyone belonged to a parish, or at least they were meant to (*see* **sturdy beggars** page 103). Thomas Cromwell ordered that the parson of each parish should keep a register of all births, marriages and deaths within the parish. These registers tell us a huge amount about life during the Tudor period.

At the centre of the parish was the church. Everyone had to go to church services or else pay a fine. The 'vestry', which meant all the men of the parish meeting together, would choose the 'church wardens'. Their job was to make sure that everyone went to church as they were supposed to. They also had to make sure that all the pubs were closed while church services were taking place.

BLOOMIN CHURCH BELLS AGAIN!

Local men had other jobs to do around the parish as well. **Elizabeth** ordered that local magistrates choose men of the vestry to be 'overseers of the poor' (*see* **poor laws**). Before that, **Mary** had ordered that each parish must have a 'surveyor of the highways' who was meant to keep the roads in good condition. Then

42

86
74

there was the beagle or local constable who patrolled the streets, to arrest wrong-doers and generally keep order. The constable was important but if he was too keen he might become unpopular with his neighbours. Men usually held these jobs part-time for one year, anyone who tried to avoid taking their turn might have to pay a large fine.

Parliament
top Tudor talking shop

In Tudor times, all major changes were authorised by acts of Parliament - 'bills' or 'acts' voted on in the Houses of Lords and Commons and 'assented' to by the king or queen. Mostly Parliaments met for quite short periods of time, when the king or queen wanted them to pass important acts - or to raise money by taxation. The most important Tudor Parliament was **Henry VIII's** Reformation Parliament (1529-36). This Parliament passed all the laws which created the Church of England and **dissolved the monasteries**.

Members of the House of Lords were - lords. Members of the House of Commons were 'gentry' the sort of men who lived in the manor house in most villages, or wealthy merchants from the towns. Poor people, most of the population, were not represented.

HEAR! HEAR!

Philip II of Spain
hard working Spanish emperor

1527-98

Philip II of Spain was a hard-working man. From a small office in his vast, gloomy palace of the Escorial outside Madrid he ruled the largest empire in Europe almost single-handed. At its height his empire included Spain, Portugal, the Netherlands, parts of Germany, parts of Italy and huge chunks of Latin America.

THAT BIT'S MINE— AND THAT, AND...

Philip was Catholic* - very Catholic. 'I do not propose or desire to be the ruler of heretics,' he told the Pope, meaning that he meant to stamp on Protestants* wherever he ruled them. In 1554 he married **Queen Mary I** because he hoped that she would make England Catholic. When Mary died, Philip backed Catholic **Mary Queen of Scots** against Protestant **Elizabeth I** (although he first tried to marry Elizabeth). He also launched the Spanish **Armada** (1588), hoping to conquer England by force.

74
72
42
10

plague
a deadly menace

Plague was a major menace throughout the Tudor period. There were two types of plague: pneumonic and bubonic. Pneumonic was deadliest. Symptoms included sweating and shivering and then black swellings. Death came quickly and was very uncomfortable.

The Tudors were ignorant of what caused illness and how to cure it. Doctors lanced the swellings to release the pus within. This was believed to be a poison and its release was believed to give the sufferer a better chance of surviving. One cure was to strap a live chicken to the wound until it died. The chicken was thought to have soaked up the illness.

Plague was incredibly infectious. There were major outbreaks in London in 1563-8, in the early 1590s and in 1603. Despite the danger of infection, large crowds of onlookers would gather to watch mass burials during epidemics.

There was little the authorities could do to stop the plague. Dogs were culled as a sanitary measure, if their owners failed to hide them. Infected houses were ordered to place placards on their doors with the words 'Lord have mercy upon us' in a red circle. The inhabitants had to stay indoors for twenty days to stop them infecting anyone else. Really, all anyone could do was to leave town or wait until the epidemic burnt itself out.

Pole, Reginald, Cardinal
✝ he burned bishops
1500-58

Reginald Pole had royal blood in his veins through his mother. That made him an important person. **Henry VIII** himself paid for Pole's education. In 1536 he became a Cardinal in the Catholic church and later he almost became Pope.

Pole was safely out of the country during the reign of Protestant* **Edward VI**. After Edward died, **Mary** made him Archbishop of Canterbury. Together Mary and Pole set about turning England back into a Catholic country again. For the next two years he was the second most important person in England. Together they arranged for the burning of nearly three hundred Protestants. He died on the same night as Mary, mission unaccomplished - England was still Protestant.

🥣 poor laws
things to do with poor people

Following the **dissolution of the monasteries** by **Henry VIII**, there was no one left to look after the poor and the weak in Tudor England. Large numbers of poor people were left to fend for themselves.

103 Henry passed fierce laws to control '**sturdy beggars**', but the problem didn't go away. Not all beggars were 'sturdy'.

In Tudor times the poor were the responsibility of
82 their local **parish**. To deal with the problem, in the
42 years 1597-8 **Elizabeth** passed a series of poor laws which told parishes what to do for their poor. Each parish had to have an 'overseer of the poor'. The overseer's job was to dish out relief to the old, the sick and the 'infant poor'. Others, those who were fit to work, were to be put to work in 'workhouses'. The overseers were to be chosen by the local magistrate.

The poor laws did something to help the lives of the poor but the workhouses were never a success. After all, most people were poor because they weren't able to work for whatever reason. The workhouses tended to fill up with old, mad and sick people and very little work got done.

Puritans
they wanted to purify the Church

Puritans were extreme Protestants*. They wanted to *purify* the Church of England of all traces of Catholicism*. They became extremely fed up when
42 **Elizabeth** moulded the Church into something moderate which even moderate Catholics could join. Puritans got the name 'Puritan' in the 1560s during

an argument about what clothes Church of England clergy ought to wear in church. They became very powerful in the following century.

NASTY PURITAN

Raleigh, Sir Walter
'the last of the Tudors'
tobacco importer, poet and soldier
around 1554-1618

42 Sir Walter Raleigh was tall, handsome, brilliant and brave. Just the sort of young man that **Elizabeth I** liked to have at her court. He had a strong Devon accent and she nicknamed him 'Water' because of the way he pronounced 'Walter'.

Raleigh was the main organiser of the first British colony in North America, which he called 'Virginia'. He was fascinated by America and is said to have introduced tobacco and the potato to England. He himself smoked a pipe. He was also a poet. Among

100
71 his friends were **Edmund Spenser**, **Christopher**
67 **Marlowe**, and perhaps **Ben Jonson** and
96 **Shakespeare**. He's said to have started their famous evenings in the Mermaid Tavern, London.

FANCY ANOTHER ONE WILL?

DON'T MIND IF I DO WALT.

Elizabeth didn't like her courtiers to fall in love with other people. Raleigh fell out of favour when he fell for her beautiful maid of honour, Elizabeth Throckmorton (1592). They married secretly but Elizabeth found out and both were briefly imprisoned.

When James I came to the throne in 1603, he accused Raleigh of conspiracy. Raleigh was locked up in the Tower of London for fifteen years - until 1618 when he was allowed out to lead an expedition to search for the fabled lost city of Eldorado, in South America (he'd tried before in 1595). The expedition failed, having burned a Spanish settlement which was against James's orders. On his return, Sir Walter, 'the last of the Tudors', was beheaded. The night before his execution he's said to have penned the lines:

> *Even such is time, that takes in trust*
> *Our youth, our joys, our all we have,*
> *And pays us but with age and dust ...*

Ridolfi Plot
banker's plan to murder Liz
1571

Roberto di Ridolfi was an Italian banker who came to live in London during the reign of **Mary**. From 1567, he was also the Pope's secret agent in England. Under cover of his banking activities, he gave money to English Catholic* conspirators and rebels.

In 1570, Ridolfi hatched a plot for a Spanish invasion of England to be combined with an uprising of English Catholics. At the same time, **Mary Queen of Scots** was to marry the **Duke of Norfolk**. **Elizabeth** would be murdered and Mary would become Queen. In March 1571, Ridolfi left for Europe to persuade the Pope and Philip II to back his scheme. His secret letters from Rome were discovered by **Cecil** and **Walsingham** and decoded. Once the plot was blown, England was no longer a safe place for Ridolfi. He had to stay on in Italy. The Duke of Norfolk was executed.

Rizzio, David

Italian secretary stabbed in Scotland

1533?-1566

Italian David Rizzio arrived in Scotland in 1561. He was about twenty-eight. At that time **Mary Queen of Scots** needed a bass voice for a quartet of singers who sang in her private chapel. Rizzio got the job.

Three years later, Mary needed a trustworthy new French secretary. Rizzio got that job too, even though his French was awful. (She had to rewrite his letters!) Next year (1565) Mary married **Lord Darnley** but soon realised that Darnley was a drunken, arrogant oaf. She relied more and more on Rizzio for advice.

He became rich and powerful and made many enemies - especially Darnley, who accused him and Mary of being lovers.

On Saturday evening 9 March 1566, Lords Morton, Ruthven and Lindsay with a gang of armed men broke into Mary's supper chamber at Holyrood Palace in Edinburgh. They dragged Rizzio away from her and stabbed him to death while Darnley stood watching. Rizzio's body bled from fifty-six dagger wounds.

Shortly after, Rizzio's job was taken by his eighteen-year-old brother Joseph. Joseph had a hand in the later murder of Darnley.

school
a tough place to learn in

A large number of people in Tudor England could read and write, not just the wealthy, and women as well as men. There were 'dame schools' in most villages where young boys and girls learned the basics. These were run by local women and cost very little. Young children of the gentry were usually taught at home.

For clever boys and boys with better off parents there were grammar schools. Many of these schools, such as Eton and Harrow, still exist today, although nowadays they're only for the rich and a few 'scholars'. In Tudor times, school started at five or six in the morning in summer, slightly later in winter, and went on till five or six at night. There were two hours for lunch. Discipline was very tough and masters expected total obedience. Beating was part of the normal school day. Punishments might include being struck on the lips or the head with a rod and being lashed in the face. Subjects included Latin and maths.

THAT HURT!

IT WAS MEANT TO!

 servants

people who knew their place - probably

There were no washing machines in Tudor times, no hoovers or fridges, microwaves or gas ovens. It took a lot of hands to run a large house, hands which belonged to the servants. Most servants were young people who had not yet got married. Well over half of all boys and half of all girls between the ages of twenty to twenty-four were servants of one kind or another.

As well as being paid their wages, servants were fed and clothed often in a 'livery' or uniform. The master and mistress were expected to look after them and to keep them in order. Servants had to call their employers 'Master (Mr) and Mistress (Mrs) Bluebottom', or whatever their surname was. (Where we get 'Mr' and Mrs' from.) Mr and Mrs Bluebottom would call their servants by their forenames.

Servants could be fined if they broke the rules:

Two pennies for not going to family prayers.

One penny for dressing untidily.

One penny for leaving a bed unmade after eight in the morning.

Six pennies for being late to serve the dinner. This seems to have been one of the worst crimes of all!

Young apprentices lived with the family like servants. They were bound to work for the master for several years. In return they learned his trade.

Seymour, Edward, Duke of Somerset 'the Good Duke'
noble protector, partly of the poor
1506?-1552

41 **Edward VI** was only nine when he came to the throne in 1547, far too young to rule. Edward Seymour was head of the 'council of regency' which ruled for him and was known as 'Lord Protector'.
95
62 Seymour's sister was **Jane Seymour**, **Henry VIII's** third wife and mother of Edward VI.

In 1549, Seymour agreed to the execution of his
22 brother Thomas, widower of **Catherine Parr**. Thomas
42 was plotting to marry the young Princess **Elizabeth** and to seize the crown when Edward VI died. With one Seymour gone, the other was bound to follow. The rest of the council decided that Edward Seymour

had to go too. He was forced from power and executed two years later.

No one was executed for their religion during Seymour's rule. Also, he tried to protect poor people from the worst effects of the **enclosures**. When he was executed, those nearest the scaffold pressed forward to dip their handkerchiefs in the blood of the 'Good Duke'.

THAT'S THE WAY. JUST LEAVE IT THERE AND LET IT SOAK UP A BIT.

Seymour, Jane

Henry's favourite queen

1509?-1537

Jane Seymour was the third wife of **Henry VIII**. He was first attracted to her in 1534/5 while he was still married to **Anne Boleyn**, his second wife. At that time Jane was Anne's lady-in-waiting and Anne became very jealous of her. On 19 May 1536, Anne was executed. Eleven days later, Jane and Henry were married. Seventeen months after that, Jane died after giving birth to the future **Edward VI**.

Jane was the best-loved of Henry's wives. He ordered that his body should be buried beside hers when his time came. Her brother **Edward Seymour, Duke of Somerset** became Lord Protector during their son Edward's short reign.

THAT POOR WOMAN— SHE'LL BE SQUASHED!

Shakespeare, William
mysterious Tudor playwright
1564-1616

William Shakespeare was probably the son of a glove maker from Stratford-on-Avon. He got married when he was eighteen, to Anne Hathaway who was eight years older than him. She was pregnant and they had twins. It's known that by 1592 he'd moved to London and had become an actor and playwright. 42 Some of his plays were acted before **Elizabeth I**. He was part-owner of the famous Globe Playhouse, now rebuilt.

Shakespeare wrote a great many plays and poems - too many to describe them all here. He seems to have been a charming man and not just a great writer. As his friend Ben Jonson described him:

> *I lov'd the man, and do honour his memory (this side Idolatry) as much as any. He was indeed honest and of an open and free nature ...*

Shakespeare bought a house back in Stratford, perhaps for his family to live in away from the dangers of London. He spent more and more time back there as he grew older and became one of the wealthiest men in the town.

EH LOOK! THAT'S WILL SHAKESPEARE!

A BIT FAT ISN'T HE?

Sidney, Sir Philip
a perfect gentleman
1554-86

Just about everyone who met Sir Philip Sidney fell in love with him. He was noble, kind and brave - and a poet. His best-loved poems are a collection of sonnets (a type of poem) called *Astrophel and Stella*, written to Penelope Devereux, daughter of the **Earl of Essex**.

In 1585 **Elizabeth I** made him governor of the Dutch town of Flushing (now Vlissingen) as part of her campaign against Catholic* Spain in the Low Countries. Next year he joined an attack on a Spanish force near the town of Zütphen further inland. The English were outnumbered six to one, but Sir Philip charged through the Spanish lines

three times. A Spanish
bullet pierced his thigh.
He had refused to wear
thigh armour. Back in camp he
handed his water bottle to a
wounded soldier saying the
famous words: 'Thy
necessity is greater than
mine.' Well perhaps not,
he died within three
weeks from an
infection of the wound.

🍵 Simnel, Lambert 🫖
he pretended to be king

around **1475-1535**

Lambert Simnel was a handsome youth from
Oxford. He had 'dignity and grace of aspect'. In
other words, he looked a bit like a royal. In 1487,
supporters of the old royal House of York wanted to
get rid of the upstart **Tudors** who had only recently
come to power (see **Henry VII**). They trained young
Lambert to pretend to be the Duke of York, one of
two 'Princes in the Tower' who had disappeared in
mysterious circumstances and who had a claim to
the throne. Later Lambert was asked to pretend to be
the Earl of Warwick instead. Warwick also had a
claim to the throne. Unfortunately, the real Earl of
Warwick was still alive and a prisoner in the Tower of
London.

In 1487, twelve-year-old Lambert/Earl of Warwick
was crowned King Edward VI in Dublin Cathedral

with a gold circlet lifted from a statue of the Virgin Mary. Meanwhile Henry VII paraded the real Earl of Warwick through the streets of London to prove that Lambert was a fake. Later that year Lambert's forces were defeated by Henry's army. Lambert was given a job in the royal kitchen and later he rose to become Henry's falconer.

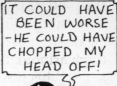

IT COULD HAVE BEEN WORSE - HE COULD HAVE CHOPPED MY HEAD OFF!

Skelton, John
poet with sharp pen
around **1460-1529**

John Skelton was 'scolemaster' to the future **Henry VIII**. Unlike most Tudor teachers, he didn't go in for beating his pupils. He didn't need to - his pen was sharp enough. He was the most famous poet of the early Tudor period. In 1502 he became Rector of Diss in Norfolk. It was in Diss that he invented 'Skeltonics' a type of poetry with short, scampering lines. Here's his description of Eleanour Rumming from Leatherhead making beer: She ...

Skimmeth it into a tray
Where the yeast is
With her maungy fystis:
And sometimes she blends
The dung of her hens
And this ale together ...

His poem, the *Boke of Phylyp Sparrow* mourns the loss of a young lady's pet (as well as mocking the funeral service). It's probably the basis for the nursery rhyme: *Who killed Cock Robin?*

Spenser, Edmund
poet of a faerie queen

around 1552-1599

Edmund Spenser loved poetry. His most famous poem is the *Faerie Queen*, published in two parts in 1589 and 1596 while he was living in Ireland. The beautiful and glorious Faerie Queen of the poem is ⁴² meant to be **Elizabeth I**. The real Elizabeth was so pleased that she granted Edmund a pension of £50 per year. Elizabeth liked a good flatterer.

Although from a noble English family, Edmund's parents were far from rich. He worked for most of his life for the English governing authority in Ireland. He was given wide acres of Irish land and became one of the English Protestant* colonists. The great ⁸¹ Irish rebellion of 1598, led by **Hugh O'Neil**, ruined him. His castle was burned while he was in it and he narrowly escaped with his life. He died in London shortly after.

sport

pointless ways to pass the time

Many of the sports which we play today were already popular in the Tudor period, although usually the rules were different.

54 *Football* was played all over the place and was often a nuisance for the authorities.

Stoolball, an ancestor of cricket, was popular in southern England.

Fives (a bit like squash, but played with the open hand) was well known.

OUCH!

62 *Tennis* was one of **Henry VIII's** favourite sports. It was an import from France. 'Tennis' comes from 'tenez', French for 'hold on'! You can see a 'real' tennis court at Henry's palace of Hampton Court. Real tennis is an early form of the game which is still played by enthusiasts.

101

Blood sports were far more popular than they are today. Hunting was a passion among the upper classes. **Elizabeth** used to have deer herded towards her so that she could shoot them with a bow and arrow while sitting in a chair.

42

Bear baiting often took place outside pubs and inns. Fierce dogs were set on the bears. Some bears such as 'Little Bess of Bromley' became stars.

Bull baiting, when bull dogs were set on captive bulls, was meant to tenderise the meat.

Bowls was fashionable and played by all classes.

Star Chamber, Court of the
a place to punish powerful men

The Court of the Star Chamber sat in a room in the Palace of Westminster, where the modern parliament building stands. It was called the Star Chamber because the ceiling was decorated with stars. It was a special court which had started back in the fourteenth century, but it was during the reign of **Henry VIII** that it came into its own. At that time, powerful men could escape the law in lesser courts. They did this by bribing judges and juries or simply by threatening them. **Thomas Wolsey** used the Star Chamber to control these 'over-mighty subjects'.

sturdy beggars
they weren't wanted

Sturdy beggars were poor people who were well enough to work but didn't. The fact that there wasn't any work for most of them was beside the point. They were a nuisance and a danger to the rich and comfortable. After the **Dissolution of the Monasteries** large gangs of sturdy beggars roamed the land, made up of out-of-work monks, and labourers who had lost their livelihoods due to the **enclosures**. Fear of sturdy beggars is remembered in the nursery rhyme:

The beggars are coming to London Town ...

Henry VIII ordered that, if caught, such 'vagabonds'

should be tied to the end of a cart and beaten until bloody. A further law of 1547 laid down that they could be made slaves for two years - and slaves for life if they ran away. Other punishments included branding with hot irons and being whipped back to their home parishes.

IS THAT BLOODY ENOUGH?

✠ Supremacy, Act of
act which removed the Pope
1534

62 When **Henry VIII** was crowned in 1509, the church in England was Catholic*. At its head was the Pope, based in Rome. Henry split with the Pope when the Pope refused to agree to Henry's divorce from his
21 first wife **Catherine of Aragon**. As a first step towards the split (1530-1), English churchmen had to agree that Henry was their Supreme Lord 'in so far as the law of Christ allows'. The Act of Supremacy of 1534 was the next step. Henry was declared 'Supreme Head on Earth of the Church of England'. There was nothing in the act about him being head only 'in so far as the law of Christ allows'.

✗ swords
long, pointed metal objects

The rapier was a long, light duelling sword first developed by the Italians. You used the point to stab your opponent rather than slashing at him with the edge. During the reign of **Elizabeth I**, the rapier was a must-have accessory for all gentlemen - and they had to know how to use it.

42

All well-brought up gentlemen took fencing lessons. They were taught to hold the rapier in their right hand, if they were right handed, and a dagger in the left hand. If they preferred they could wear a thick leather glove on the left hand instead of carrying a dagger. To make sure that fights were fair, a law of 1580 limited the length of swords to three feet (91.44 cm) and the length of daggers to one foot (30.48 cm).

Duels could be incredibly bloody. A duel of the reign of **Henry VIII** describes both contestants dripping with blood and the victor dying over his opponent's blood-soaked, dead body.

62

Meanwhile, the old-fashioned English style of sword fighting, with a strong broad sword in the right hand

and a buckler, or small shield on the left arm, was kept alive by professional swordsmen. There was more slashing and wrestling in old-style sword fighting. The professionals formed a company and used to give shows or contests to the paying public, usually in inn yards, where the first Tudor plays were put on as well (*see* **theatre**).

theatre
blood, thunder and beautiful words

Tudor theatre was extraordinary. Some of the greatest writers of all time, such as **Shakespeare** and **Marlowe**, created some of the greatest works ever written for it. Nothing quite like it had ever happened before. It had its roots in Medieval 'mystery' plays but this was combined with ideas taken from the plays of ancient Greece.

96

71

Large numbers of Londoners flocked to the theatre. To start with, plays were performed in the courtyards of large inns but soon proper theatres were built. The first was the 'Theatre' (1576) which could hold up to a thousand. Others soon followed, including Shakespeare's Globe, first built in 1599 from bits of the old Theatre. The largest theatres could hold over three thousand.

Plays were staged in the afternoon. After a leisurely lunch, citizens who had the time and the money would make their way to a theatre around 2.00 pm, for the start of the performance. Some of the theatres, including the Globe, were on the south bank of the Thames. This was the entertainment area of London because it was beyond reach of the city authorities. Theatre-goers would usually cross the river by boat, the main form of transport in Tudor London.

Audiences fell silent if the play was good, but they would hiss and boo and throw things if they didn't like what they saw. To keep them happy, before and after a play there might be other entertainments such as dog fights or bear baiting. Plays themselves were as exciting as possible with plenty of blood and sound effects.

Drummers made thunder.

Three vials of blood and a sheep's gather [lungs, liver and heart]. (For a torture scene.)

BOOM!

Stage battles were fought to the sound of real cannons and guns. Battles at the GlobeTheatre could be heard right across the Thames in the City of London.

Rain effects were made by throwing down dried peas.

From the very start, Tudor theatre came under attack

87 from **Puritans**. They claimed that the theatres tempted young workmen and apprenticies to be idle. Certainly, theatres were quite lawless places. There were always plenty of sword-wielding young toughs in the 'pit', ready to pick a fight. The pit was the cheap, standing area in front of the stage.

Fortunately for our language, theatre was protected by some of the most powerful people in the land.

42 **Elizabeth** liked to watch plays, as did her favourite
39 the **Earl of Leicester**. The Earl of Oxford formed his own company of 'players' back in 1547.

✚ Thirty-Nine Articles
what priests had to believe in
1571

What is the Church of England? Can anyone belong? Well, in the reign of **Elizabeth**, everyone *had* to belong, whether Protestant* or Catholic* or secret worshipper of the Great God Bloggerdomp. The Thirty-Nine Articles were a statement of what they had to believe in. The Articles were drawn up by the Church itself and all Church of England clergy had to accept them - or else.

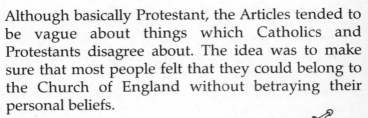

Although basically Protestant, the Articles tended to be vague about things which Catholics and Protestants disagree about. The idea was to make sure that most people felt that they could belong to the Church of England without betraying their personal beliefs.

Throckmorton Plot 🗡
Catholic plan to replace Liz
1583

The Throckmorton Plot was dreamt up by the Duke of Guise, a French relative of **Mary Queen of Scots**. There would be a Catholic* invasion of England and Scotland (at the same time) and an uprising of English Catholics. Mary Queen of Scots would become Queen of both countries, and Protestant* **Elizabeth** would be got rid of.

Walsingham got wind of the plot. He put a spy called Fagot in the French Embassy in London. Fagot reported that Francis Throckmorton, an English Catholic, was visiting the embassy secretly at night. Throckmorton was arrested and twice tortured on the rack. His confession gave away details of the Plot and papers were found in his room with plans of possible landing sites for a French army. He was executed.

toilets
an earthy subject

In Tudor times, most toilets were earth toilets. The toilet might just be a mound close to the back door of a cottage. More often however, toilet seats were placed over a pit. Instead of flushing the toilet with water, earth was scattered to stop smells. In smarter houses the pit would be a cellar, cleared out occasionally by a man with a shovel.

MUM! WE'RE OUT OF EARTH!

FETCH A SPADE THEN!

Two toilet seats might be placed side by side for greater convenience. There might also be another, smaller seat with a bucket beneath. This was to collect urine. Urine was an ingredient of 'lye', which was used to wash clothes.

The Tudors were much less prudish than we are today:

You may rise in dinner-time to ask for a close-stool. You may invite some special friend of yours from the table to hold discourse with you as you sit in the withdrawing-chamber.

The 'water closet' was invented by Sir John Harington (1561-1612), beloved but wild godson of **Elizabeth I**, and it was a great improvement. He published his design in *A New Discourse upon a Stale Subject* (1596). The subtitle was *The Metamorphosis (changing) of Ajax*. 'Ajax' being a play on 'jakes', the Tudor word for a toilet. Elizabeth banned Harington from court (for the second time) because the book made rude fun of important courtiers, including her favourite the **Earl of Leicester**. But Harington was soon forgiven. In 1598, the first ever modern water closet was installed, for Elizabeth's use, at Richmond Palace.

🫖 Tudors
they might have been Merediths

For a royal family, the Tudors had a very weak claim to the throne of England. **Henry VII**, the first Tudor king, inherited his claim through his mother Margaret Beaufort. Margaret had royal blood in her veins - but only via the third son of Edward III, called John of Gaunt (1340-99), and John's mistress, Katherine Swynford.

Margaret Beaufort had married Henry VII's father Edmund Tudor in 1455 when she was only twelve. She gave birth to the future Henry VII before she was fourteen so she wasn't much older than her son. They were always close friends.

Henry's father Edmund Tudor was the Earl of Richmond. But his father's father, Owen Tudor (also spelled Tydier, Tidir and Tudur) was an upstart. Owen was a Welsh squire. His full name was Owen ap Meredith ap Tudor, 'ap' being Welsh for 'son of' (so the Tudors could equally well have been called the 'Merediths').

KING HENRY MEREDITH

Around 1429, Owen Tudor had married the French princess Catherine of Valois (the widow of the English king Henry V and mother of Henry VI of England). Owen and Catherine of Valois married secretly, because he wasn't of royal descent.

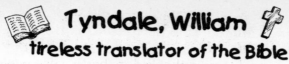

Tyndale, William ✝
tireless translator of the Bible
around 1492-1536

William Tyndale was an early English Protestant*. He studied under Martin Luther, the great German priest who founded Protestantism and he believed that all English people should have the chance to read the Bible for themselves. Under Luther's influence, Tyndale translated the Bible into English directly from the ancient Latin, Greek and Hebrew. His Bible is one of the greatest works of literature in the English language. It's the foundation stone of the famous 'Authorised' version of 1611.

For most of his life Tyndale had to live on the continent because England was too dangerous for him. In 1531, **Henry VIII** tried to have him kidnapped and brought home to stand trial as a heretic. Finally in 1535, he was captured in Antwerp by Catholic* agents of Emperor Charles V. Eighteen months later he was burned at the stake having first been strangled.

> I DIE, BUT MY WORDS LIVE ON!

62

Uniformity, Acts of *see* **Common Prayer, Book of**

Union, Act of
when England and Wales got together
1536

112 The **Tudors** were a Welsh family so they always took a close interest in Wales. Wales had been ruled by

English kings since 1284, but had always been treated differently. In the Act of Union of 1536, **Henry VIII** declared that he wanted Wales to be fully a part of his kingdom. The Act gave Welshmen political equality with Englishmen. For the first time, the Welsh could send Welsh MPs to Parliament, and English common law was to be used in Welsh courts rather than Welsh law.

villains
nasty people who steal things

Tudor England was not a safe place. Honest citizens did not venture out onto the streets at night if they could avoid it. It was sensible to hire a 'link-boy' with a torch to light you home. Every householder in London was meant to hang a lantern outside his house at night, but solitary candles behind horn can't have done much to lighten the gloom. At night the watchman would call:

Twelve O'clock, look well to your locks,
Your fire and your light,
And so good night.

There were many different types of crook:

Anglers used long poles with a hook on the end to steal valuables through open windows.

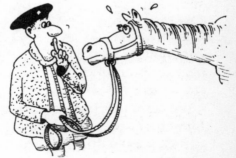

Upright men were the leaders of criminal gangs.

Priggers stole horses.

Doxies were prostitutes and the womenfolk of criminals.

Cyrtsey men pretended to be gentry fallen on hard times.

Cutpurses cut the strings with which people tied their purses to their belts.

Kinchin morts were little girls brought up to steal.

Prison wasn't a common punishment; beating, branding, the stocks and the pillory were more common, but even so there had to be somewhere to lock people up.

There were five prisons on the south bank of the Thames: the Kig's Bench, the White Lion, the Counter, the Marshalsea and - the Clink.

Walsingham, Sir Francis
top Tudor spy master

1532-90

From 1568 until his death twenty-two years later, Walsingham was one of the most powerful members of the government of **Elizabeth I**. He ran what might be called her Foreign Office. To help him in his task, he created one of the most efficient secret services in Europe - and paid for it out of his own pocket. At one time he had fifty-three agents in the courts of Europe plus many spies. It was thanks to Sir Francis as much as anyone that Elizabeth survived so many plots against her life.

Walsingham often disagreed with Elizabeth. She liked to play for time and avoid making decisions for as long as possible. Walsingham was more hasty. Despite this, he always did what Elizabeth wanted him to do eventually. She trusted him.

Walsingham had a beautiful daughter. She married **Sir Philip Sidney** and after he died, **Robert Devereux, the Earl of Essex**. He died poor, having spent all his fortune on his secret service.

117

🍵 Warbeck, Perkin 🫖
handsome royal pretender
around 1474-1499

In 1491 Perkin (Peter) Warbeck landed in Cork, Ireland. He was wearing, or perhaps modelling, the costly clothes of his employer, a merchant from Brittany called Pregent Meno. Perkin looked so good that people thought that he must really be a nobleman - or better. To cut a long story short, Perkin pretended that he was Richard Duke of York, one of the 'Princes in the Tower' who had mysteriously disappeared some years before. As such he had a claim to the crown of **Henry VII**, the first Tudor king of England.

Perkin was recognised as 'Richard IV of England' by European kings, and he married a cousin of James IV of Scotland. After several attempts to invade England, he was captured by Henry's forces (1497).

Henry was merciful. He allowed Perkin to remain at his court although closely watched. But first, Perkin had to confess who he really was to his wife (he was actually the son of a customs official from Tournai in the Netherlands). She was naturally very upset. Perkin then made several attempts to escape and was finally hanged at Tyburn (now Marble Arch).

61

Wolsey, Thomas
'Cardinal Wolsey'
lavish Lord Chancellor to Henry VIII

around **1475-1530**

From humble beginnings Thomas Wolsey rose to become Lord Chancellor of England under **Henry VIII** and a Cardinal, the highest job in the Catholic* Church after Pope. From 1515-29 he was the second most powerful man in England. He never travelled without hundreds of servants following behind, and foreign rulers treated him almost as a fellow king. He also became incredibly rich. His annual income was said to be as much as a quarter of Henry's - and Henry was meant to have enough to run the entire country! Not bad for a butcher's son from Ipswich.

Wolsey built Hampton Court Palace, which he later gave to Henry. He founded Christ's Church College in Oxford and a school in Ipswich (where he came from). But his doom was sealed when he failed to persuade the Pope to agree to Henry's divorce from his first wife **Catherine of Aragon**. He died while under arrest for high treason on the road from York to London. His last words were:

If I had served God as diligently as I have done the King, he would not have given me over in my grey hairs.

women

people who wore skirts

Paradise for women, purgatory for men and a hell for horses.

That's how one Italian traveller described Tudor England. He was amazed by the free lifestyle of the wives of wealthy London merchants. It seemed to him that they spent their time chatting with friends or going out and about in fine clothes. Italian women would have been at home looking after their families.

Certainly, English women enjoyed more freedom than women in many other countries, but they weren't free by modern standards. Daughters were brought up to be wives, and once married they were firmly under the control of their husbands. The husband controlled the property and the wife couldn't even make a will without his permission. Which is not to say that marriages were unhappy. All the evidence suggests that husbands and wives loved each other as much, or sometimes as little, as they do nowadays.

Couples tended to wait to get married until they could afford to set up home together. For women, that meant that they got married at an average age of around twenty-five. Noble women however were married young, and their marriages were arranged by their fathers. They themselves had very little to do with the decision.

Perhaps the main difference between the lives of women then and now, both noble and common, was the sheer number of children they had. Married women spent most of their time either pregnant or nursing young babies.

GLOSSARY

ALCHEMY: the study of how to turn cheaper metals into gold. It involved more magic than science and wasn't actually possible. Despite this, in some ways, alchemy was a forerunner of modern chemistry.

ASTROLOGY: The 'science' of judging a person's character and even of trying to predict his or her future from the position of stars. There's no evidence that astrology works but it was widely believed in Tudor times.

CATHOLICS: Catholics are members of the Roman Catholic Church and the Pope is their leader. Nearly everyone in Western Europe was a Catholic until the early sixteenth century. Catholic services were conducted in Latin and the Bible was read in Latin.

PROTESTANTS: By the early sixteenth century the Catholic Church had become corrupt. A German monk, Martin Luther (1483-1546), started the 'Reformation' to try to reform the Church. All kinds of breakaway movements followed. The breakaway churches refused to obey the Pope and their followers became known as Protestants. Protestants conducted their services in their native languages and allowed their priests to marry.

WARS OF THE ROSES: For thirty years (1455-85) on and off, two families with royal blood battled it out for the crown of England. On one side was the House of Lancaster, symbol a white rose, on the other side was the House of York, symbol a red rose: thus the 'Wars of the Roses'. By beating the Yorkists and then marrying Elizabeth of York, Henry VII finally stopped the wars.

INDEX

NOW READ ON

If you want to know more about the Tudors, see if your local library or bookshop has this book.

WHAT THEY DON'T TELL YOU ABOUT THE TUDORS
By Bob Fowke (Hodder Children's Books 1995). A big, fat, funny book featuring wife-specialist, greedy pig and great king Henry VIII, poor, young and fairly-feeble Edward VI, fanatical, eyebrowless and rather sad Mary I plus (saving the best for last) the great Elizabeth I.

This book gives you the low-down on sixteenth century Britain in all its gory detail - and it also tells the story of how the Tudors took power and held onto it, all in a funny but sensible way. By the time you've finished, you'll have a good idea of the politics and passions of the time - but you may just be pleased to find yourself back in the twenty-first century when you finally close the covers!

ABOUT THE AUTHOR

Bob Fowke is a well-known author of children's information books. Writing under various pen names and with various friends and colleagues, he has created many unusual and entertaining works on all manner of subjects.

There's always more to his books than meets the eye - look at all the entries in the index of this one!

Who? What? When?
ORDER FORM

0 340 85185 6	TUDORS	£4.99
0 340 85184 8	VICTORIANS	£4.99
0 340 85186 4	WORLD WAR I	£4.99
0 340 85187 2	WORLD WAR II	£4.99

All Hodder Children's books are available at your local bookshop or newsagent, or can be ordered direct from the publisher. Just write to the address below. Prices and availability subject to change without notice.

Hodder Children's Books, Cash Sales Department, Bookpoint, 130 Milton Park, Abingdon, Oxon, OX14 4SB, UK.
Email address: orders@bookpoint.co.uk

Please enclose a cheque or postal order made payable to Bookpoint Ltd to the value of the cover price and allow the following for postage and packing:
UK & BFPO - £1.00 for the first book, 50p for the second book, and 30p for each additional book ordered, up to a maximum charge of £3.00. OVERSEAS & EIRE - £2.00 for the first book, £1.00 for the second book, and 50p for each additional book.

If you have a credit card you may order by telephone - (01235) 400414 (lines open 9am-6pm, Monday to Saturday; 24 hour message answering service). Alternatively you can send a fax on 01235 400454.